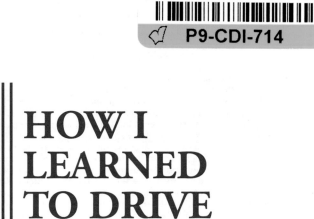

HOW I LEARNED TO DRIVE
BY PAULA VOGEL

★ Revised Edition

★

DRAMATISTS
PLAY SERVICE
INC.

2

This play is dedicated to Peter Franklin.

HOW I LEARNED TO DRIVE was produced by Vineyard Theatre (Douglas Aibel, Artistic Director; Jon Nakagawa, Managing Director) in New York City in February, 1997. It was directed by Mark Brokaw; the set design was by Narelle Sissons; the costume design was by Jess Goldstein; the lighting design was by Mark McCullough; the original sound design was by David van Tieghem; and the production stage manager was Thea Bradshaw Gillies. The cast was as follows:

LI'L BIT ....Mary-Louise Parker
PECK...David Morse
MALE GREEK CHORUS ....Michael Showalter
FEMALE GREEK CHORUS ....Johanna Day
TEENAGE GREEK CHORUS.............................Kerry O'Malley

The Vineyard Theatre production, in association with Daryl Roth and Roy Gabay, moved to the Century Theatre, in New York City, in April, 1997. MALE GREEK CHORUS was played by Christopher Duva.

This play was made possible by generous support from the Pew Charitable Trust and the John Simon Guggenheim Foundation. It was written and developed at the Perseverance Theatre, Juneau, Alaska; Molly Smith, Artistic Director.

CHARACTERS

LI'L BIT — A woman who ages forty-something to eleven years old. (See Notes on the New York Production.)

PECK — Attractive man in his forties. Despite a few problems, he should be played by an actor one might cast in the role of Atticus in *To Kill A Mockingbird.*

THE GREEK CHORUS If possible, these three members should be able to sing three-part harmony.

> MALE GREEK CHORUS — Plays Grandfather, Waiter, High School Boys. Thirties-forties. (See Notes on the New York Production.)

> FEMALE GREEK CHORUS — Plays Mother, Aunt Mary, High School Girls. Thirty-fifty. (See Notes on the New York Production.)

> TEENAGE GREEK CHORUS — Plays Grandmother, High School Girls, and the voice of eleven-year-old Li'l Bit. Note on the casting of this actor: I would strongly recommend casting a young woman who is "of legal age," that is, twenty-one to twenty-five years old who can look as close to eleven as possible. The contrast with the other cast members will help. If the actor is too young, the audience may feel uncomfortable. (See Notes on the New York Production.)

PRODUCTION NOTES

I urge directors to use the Greek Chorus in staging as environment and, well, part of the family — with the exception of the Teenage Greek Chorus member who, after the last time she appears onstage, should perhaps disappear.

As for music: please have fun. I wrote sections of the play listening to music like Roy Orbison's "Dream Baby"* and the Mamas and the Papa's "Dedicated to the One I Love."* The vaudeville sections go well to Tijuana Brass* or any music that sounds like a *Laugh-In* soundtrack.* Other sixties music is rife with pedophilish (?) reference: The Beach Boys "Little Surfer Girl,"* the "You're Sixteen" genre hits; "Come Back When You Grow Up, Girl"* Gary Pickett and the Union Gap's "This Girl Is a Woman Now,"* etc.

Don't forget that all rights must be obtained before using specific music in your production.

And whenever possible, please feel free to punctuate the action with traffic signs: "No Passing," "Slow Children," "Dangerous Curves," "One Way," and the visual signs for children, deer crossings, hills, school buses, etc. (see Notes on the New York Production).

ON TITLES

Throughout the script there are bold-faced titles. In production these should be spoken in a neutral voice (the type of voice that driver education films employ). In the New York production these titles were assigned to various members of the Greek Chorus and were done live.

* See Special Note on Songs and Recordings on copyright page.

NOTES ON THE NEW YORK PRODUCTION

The role of Li'l Bit was originally written as a character who is forty-something. When we cast Mary-Louise Parker in the role of Li'l Bit, we cast the Greek Chorus members with younger actors as the Female Greek and the Male Greek, and cast the Teenage Greek with an older (that is, mid-twenties) actor as well. There is a great deal of flexibility in age. Directors should change the age in the last monologue for Li'l Bit ("And before you know it, I'll be thirty-five") to reflect the actor's age who is playing Li'l Bit.

This script uses the notion of slides and projections, which were not used in the New York production of the play.

HOW I LEARNED TO DRIVE

As the house lights dim, a Voice announces:

Safety first — You and Driver Education.

Then the sound of a key turning the ignition of a car. Li'l Bit steps into a spotlight on the stage; "well-endowed," she is a softer-looking woman in the present time than she was at seventeen.

LI'L BIT.   Sometimes to tell a secret, you first have to teach a lesson. We're going to start our lesson tonight on an early, warm summer evening.

In a parking lot overlooking the Beltsville Agricultural Farms in suburban Maryland.

Less than a mile away, the crumbling concrete of U.S. One winds its way past one-room revival churches, the porno drive-in, and boarded up motels with For Sale signs tumbling down.

Like I said, it's a warm summer evening.

Here on the land the Department of Agriculture owns, the smell of sleeping farm animal is thick on the air. The smells of clover and hay mix in with the smells of the leather dashboard. You can still imagine how Maryland used to be, before the malls took over. This countryside was once dotted with farmhouses — from their porches you could have witnessed the Civil War raging in the front fields.

Oh yes. There's a moon over Maryland tonight, that spills into the car where I sit beside a man old enough to be — did I mention how still the night is? Damp soil and tranquil air. It's the kind of night that makes a middle-aged man with a mortgage feel like a country boy again.

It's 1969. And I am very old, very cynical of the world, and I know it all. In short, I am seventeen years old, parking off a dark lane with a married man on an early summer night. *(Lights up on two chairs facing front — or a Buick Riviera, if you will. Waiting patiently, with a smile on his face, Peck sits sniffing the night air. Li'l Bit climbs in beside him, seventeen years old and tense. Throughout the following, the two sit facing directly front. They do not touch. Their bodies remain passive. Only their facial expressions emote.)*

PECK.   Ummm. I love the smell of your hair.

LI'L BIT.   Uh-huh.

PECK.   Oh, Lord. Ummmm. *(Beat.)* A man could die happy like this.

LI'L BIT.   Well, *don't.*

PECK.   What shampoo is this?

LI'L BIT.   Herbal Essence.

PECK.   Herbal Essence. I'm gonna buy me some. Herbal Essence. And when I'm all alone in the house, I'm going to get into the bathtub, and uncap the bottle and —

LI'L BIT.   — Be good.

PECK.   What?

LI'L BIT.   Stop being ... bad.

PECK.   What did you think I was going to say? What do you think I'm going to do with the shampoo?

LI'L BIT.   I don't want to know. I don't want to hear it.

PECK.   I'm going to wash my hair. That's all.

LI'L BIT.   Oh.

PECK.   What did you think I was going to do?

LI'L BIT.   Nothing ... I don't know. Something ... nasty.

PECK.   With shampoo? Lord, gal — your mind!

LI'L BIT.   And whose fault is it?

PECK.   Not mine. I've got the mind of a boy scout.

LI'L BIT.   Right. A horny boy scout.

PECK.   Boy scouts are always horny. What do you think the first Merit Badge is for?

LI'L BIT.   There. You're going to be nasty again.

PECK.   Oh, no. I'm good. Very good.

LI'L BIT.   It's getting late.

PECK.   Don't change the subject. I was talking about how good I am. *(Beat.)* Are you ever gonna let me show you how good I am?

LI'L BIT.   Don't go over the line now.

10

PECK. I won't. I'm not gonna do anything you don't want me to do.

LI'L BIT. That's right.

PECK. And I've been good all week.

LI'L BIT. You have?

PECK. Yes. All week. Not a single drink.

LI'L BIT. Good boy.

PECK. Do I get a reward? For not drinking?

LI'L BIT. A small one. It's getting late.

PECK. Just let me undo you. I'll do you back up.

LI'L BIT. All right. But be quick about it. *(Peck pantomimes undoing Li'l Bit's brassiere with one hand.)* You know, that's amazing. The way you can undo the hooks through my blouse with one hand.

PECK. Years of practice.

LI'L BIT. You would make an incredible brain surgeon with that dexterity.

PECK. I'll bet Clyde — what's the name of the boy taking you to the prom?

LI'L BIT. Claude Souders.

PECK. Claude Souders. I'll bet it takes him two hands, lights on, and you helping him on to get to first base.

LI'L BIT. Maybe. *(Beat.)*

PECK. Can I ... kiss them? Please?

LI'L BIT. I don't know.

PECK. Don't make a grown man beg.

LI'L BIT. Just one kiss.

PECK. I'm going to lift your blouse.

LI'L BIT. It's a little cold. *(Peck laughs gently.)*

PECK. That's not why you're shivering. *(They sit, perfectly still, for a long moment of silence. Peck makes gentle, concentric circles with his thumbs in the air in front of him.)* How does that feel? *(Li'l Bit closes her eyes, carefully keeps her voice calm.)*

LI'L BIT. It's ... okay. *(Sacred music, organ music or a boy's choir swells beneath the following.)*

PECK. I tell you, you can keep all the cathedrals of Europe. Just give me a second with these — these celestial orbs — *(Peck*

11

bows his head as if praying. But he is kissing her nipple. Li'l Bit, eyes still closed, rears back her head on the leather Buick car seat.)

LI'L BIT.   Uncle Peck — we've got to go. I've got graduation rehearsal at school tomorrow morning. And you should get on home to Aunt Mary —

PECK.   — All right, Li'l Bit.

LI'L BIT.   — *Don't* call me that no more. *(Calmer.)* Any more. I'm a big girl now, Uncle Peck. As you know. *(Li'l Bit pantomimes refastening her bra behind her back.)*

PECK.   That you are. Going on eighteen. Kittens will turn into cats. *(Sighs.)* I live all week long for these few minutes with you — you know that?

LI'L BIT.   I'll drive.

(A Voice cuts in with:)

Idling in the Neutral Gear.

(Sound of car revving cuts off the sacred music; Li'l Bit, now an adult, rises out of the car and comes to us.)

LI'L BIT.   In most families, relatives get names like "Junior," or "Brother," or "Bubba." In my family, if we call someone "Big Papa," it's not because he's tall. In my family, folks tend to get nicknamed for their genitalia. Uncle Peck, for example. My mama's adage was "the titless wonder," and my cousin Bobby got branded for life as "B.B." *(In unison with Greek Chorus:)*

LI'L BIT.	GREEK CHORUS.
For blue balls.	For blue balls.

FEMALE GREEK CHORUS.   *(As Mother.)* And of course, we were so excited to have a baby girl that when the nurse brought you in and said, "It's a girl! It's a baby girl!" I just had to see for myself. So we whipped your diapers down and parted your chubby little legs — and right between your legs there was — *(Peck has come over during the above and chimes along:)*

PECK.	GREEK CHORUS.
Just a little bit.	Just a little bit.

FEMALE GREEK CHORUS.   *(As Mother.)* And when you were born, you were so tiny that you fit in Uncle Peck's outstretched hand. *(Peck stretches his hand out.)*

PECK.   Now that's a fact. I held you, one day old, right in this hand. *(A traffic signal is projected of a bicycle in a circle with a diagonal red slash.)*

LI'L BIT.   Even with my family background, I was sixteen or so before I realized that pedophilia did not mean people who loved to bicycle ...

(A Voice intrudes:)

Driving in First Gear.

LI'L BIT.   1969. A typical family dinner.

FEMALE GREEK CHORUS.   *(As Mother.)* Look, Grandma. Li'l Bit's getting to be as big in the bust as you are.

LI'L BIT.   Mother! Could we please change the subject?

TEENAGE GREEK CHORUS.   *(As Grandmother.)* Well, I hope you are buying her some decent bras. I never had a decent bra, growing up in the Depression, and now my shoulders are just crippled — crippled from the weight hanging on my shoulders — the dents from my bra straps are big enough to put your finger in. — Here, let me show you — *(As Grandmother starts to open her blouse:)*

LI'L BIT.   Grandma! Please don't undress at the dinner table.

PECK.   I thought the entertainment came *after* the dinner.

LI'L BIT.   *(To the audience.)* This is how it always starts. My grandfather, Big Papa, will chime in next with —

MALE GREEK CHORUS.   *(As Grandfather.)* Yup. If Li'l Bit gets any bigger, we're gonna haveta buy her a wheelbarrow to carry in front of her —

LI'L BIT.   — Damn it —

PECK.   — How about those Redskins on Sunday, Big Papa?

LI'L BIT.   *(To the audience.)* The only sport Big Papa followed was chasing Grandma around the house —

MALE GREEK CHORUS.   *(As Grandfather.)* — Or we could write to Kate Smith. Ask her for somma her used brassieres she don't want anymore — she could maybe give to Li'l Bit here —

LI'L BIT.   — I can't stand it. I can't.

PECK.   Now, honey, that's just their way —

FEMALE GREEK CHORUS.   *(As Mother.)* I tell you, Grandma, Li'l Bit's at that age. She's so sensitive, you can't say boo —

LI'L BIT.   I'd like some privacy, that's all. Okay? Some god-damn privacy —

PECK. — Well, at least she didn't use the Savior's name —

LI'L BIT. *(To the audience.)* And Big Papa wouldn't let a dead dog lie. No sirree.

MALE GREEK CHORUS. *(As Grandfather.)* Well, she'd better stop being so sensitive. 'Cause five minutes before Li'l Bit turns the corner, her tits turn first —

LI'L BIT. *(Starting to rise from the table.)* — That's it. That's it.

PECK. Li'l Bit, you can't let him get to you. Then he wins.

LI'L BIT. I hate him. *Hate* him.

PECK. That's fine. But hate him and eat a good dinner at the same time. *(Li'l Bit calms down and sits with perfect dignity.)*

LI'L BIT. The gumbo is really good, Grandma.

MALE GREEK CHORUS. *(As Grandfather.)* A'course, Li'l Bit's got a big surprise coming for her when she goes to that fancy college this fall —

PECK. Big Papa — let it go.

MALE GREEK CHORUS. *(As Grandfather.)* What does she need a college degree for? She's got all the credentials she'll need on her chest —

LI'L BIT. — Maybe I want to learn things. Read. Rise above my cracker background —

PECK. — Whoa, now, Li'l Bit —

MALE GREEK CHORUS. *(As Grandfather.)* What kind of things do you want to read?

LI'L BIT. There's a whole semester course, for example, on Shakespeare — *(Male Greek Chorus, as Grandfather, laughs until he weeps.)*

MALE GREEK CHORUS. *(As Grandfather.)* Shakespeare. That's a good one. Shakespeare is really going to help you in life.

PECK. I think it's wonderful. And on scholarship!

MALE GREEK CHORUS. *(As Grandfather.)* How is Shakespeare going to help her lie on her back in the dark? *(Li'l Bit is on her feet.)*

LI'L BIT. You're getting old, Big Papa. You are going to die — very very soon. Maybe even *tonight*. And when you get to heaven, God's going to be a beautiful black woman in a long white robe. She's gonna look at your chart and say: Uh-oh. Fornication. Dog-ugly mean with blood relatives. Oh. Uh-oh.

Voted for George Wallace. Well, one last chance: If you can name the play, all will be forgiven. And then she'll quote: "The quality of mercy is not strained." Your answer? Oh, too bad — *Merchant of Venice:* Act IV, Scene iii. And then she'll send your ass to fry in hell with all the other crackers. Excuse me, please.

(To the audience.) And as I left the house, I would always hear Big Papa say:

MALE GREEK CHORUS. *(As Grandfather.)* Lucy, your daughter's got a mouth on her. Well, no sense in wasting good gumbo. Pass me her plate, Mama.

LI'L BIT. And Aunt Mary would come up to Uncle Peck:

FEMALE GREEK CHORUS. *(As Aunt Mary.)* Peck, go after her, will you? You're the only one she'll listen to when she gets like this.

PECK. She just needs to cool off.

FEMALE GREEK CHORUS. *(As Aunt Mary.)* Please, honey — Grandma's been on her feet cooking all day.

PECK. All right.

LI'L BIT. And as he left the room, Aunt Mary would say:

FEMALE GREEK CHORUS. *(As Aunt Mary.)* Peck's so good with them when they get to be this age. *(Li'l Bit has stormed to another part of the stage, her back turned, weeping with a teenage fury. Peck, cautiously, as if stalking a deer, comes to her. She turns away even more. He waits a bit.)*

PECK. I don't suppose you're talking to family. *(No response.)* Does it help that I'm in-law?

LI'L BIT. Don't you dare make fun of this.

PECK. I'm not. There's nothing funny about this. *(Beat.)* Although I'll bet when Big Papa is about to meet his maker, he'll remember *The Merchant of Venice.*

LI'L BIT. I've got to get away from here.

PECK. You're going away. Soon. Here, take this. *(Peck hands her his folded handkerchief. Li'l Bit uses it, noisily. Hands it back. Without her seeing, he reverently puts it back.)*

LI'L BIT. I hate this family.

PECK. Your grandfather's ignorant. And you're right — he's going to die soon. But he's family. Family is ... family.

LI'L BIT. Grown-ups are always saying that. Family.

15

PECK. Well, when you get a little older, you'll see what we're saying.

LI'L BIT. Uh-huh. So family is another acquired taste, like French kissing?

PECK. Come again?

LI'L BIT. You know, at first it really grosses you out, but in time you grow to like it?

PECK. Girl, you are ... a handful.

LI'L BIT. Uncle Peck — you have the keys to your car?

PECK. Where do you want to go?

LI'L BIT. Just up the road.

PECK. I'll come with you.

LI'L BIT. No — please? I just need to ... to drive for a little bit. Alone. *(Peck tosses her the keys.)*

PECK. When can I see you alone again?

LI'L BIT. Tonight. *(Li'l Bit crosses to C. while the lights dim around her.*

A Voice directs:)

Shifting Forward from First to Second Gear.

LI'L BIT. There were a lot of rumors about why I got kicked out of that fancy school in 1970. Some say I got caught with a man in my room. Some say as a kid on scholarship I fooled around with a rich man's daughter. *(Li'l Bit smiles innocently at the audience.)*

I'm not talking.

But the real truth was I had a constant companion in my dorm room — who was less than discrete. Canadian V.O. A fifth a day.

1970. A Nixon recession. I slept on the floors of friends who were out of work themselves. Took factory work when I could find it. A string of dead-end day jobs that didn't last very long.

What I did, most nights, was cruise the Beltway and the back roads of Maryland, where there was still country, past the battlefields and farm houses. Racing in a 1965 Mustang — and as long as I had gasoline for my car and whiskey for me, the nights would pass. Fully tanked, I would speed past the churches and the trees on the bend, thinking just one notch of the steering wheel would be all it would take, and yet some ... reflex

16

took over. My hands on the wheel in the nine and three o'clock position — I never so much as got a ticket. He taught me well. *(A Voice announces:)*

You and the Reverse Gear.

LI'L BIT.   Back up. 1968. On the Eastern Shore. A celebration dinner. *(Li'l Bit joins Peck at a table in a restaurant.)*

PECK.   Feeling better, missy?

LI'L BIT.   The bathroom's really amazing here, Uncle Peck! They have these little soaps — instead of borax or something — and they're in the shape of shells.

PECK.   I'll have to take a trip to the gentleman's room just to see.

LI'L BIT.   How did you know about this place?

PECK.   This inn is famous on the Eastern Shore — it's been open since the seventeenth century. And I know how you like history … *(Li'l Bit is shy and pleased.)*

LI'L BIT.   It's great.

PECK.   And you've just done your first, legal, long-distance drive. You must be hungry.

LI'L BIT.   I'm starved.

PECK.   I would suggest a dozen oysters to start, and the crab imperial … *(Li'l Bit is genuinely agog.)* You might be interested to know the town history. When the British sailed up this very river in the dead of night — see outside where I'm pointing? — they were going to bombard the heck out of this town. But the town fathers were ready for them. They crept up all the trees with lanterns so that the British would think they saw the town lights and they aimed their cannons too high. And that's why the inn is still here for business today.

LI'L BIT.   That's a great story.

PECK.   *(Casually.)* Would you like to start with a cocktail?

LI'L BIT.   You're not … you're not going to start drinking, are you, Uncle Peck?

PECK.   Not me. I told you, as long as you're with me, I'll never drink. I asked you if *you'd* like a cocktail before dinner. It's nice to have a little something with the oysters.

LI'L BIT.   But … I'm not … legal. We could get arrested. Uncle Peck, they'll never believe I'm twenty-one!

PECK. So? Today we celebrate your driver's license — on the first try. This establishment reminds me a lot of places back home.

LI'L BIT. What does that mean?

PECK. In South Carolina, like here on the Eastern Shore, they're ... *(Searches for the right euphemism.)* ... "European." Not so puritanical. And very understanding if gentlemen wish to escort very attractive young ladies who might want a before-dinner cocktail. If you want one, I'll order one.

LI'L BIT. Well — sure. Just ... one. *(The Female Greek Chorus appears in a spot.)*

FEMALE GREEK CHORUS. *(As Mother.)* A Mother's Guide to Social Drinking:

A lady never gets sloppy — she may, however, get tipsy and a little gay.

Never drink on an empty stomach. Avail yourself of the bread basket and generous portions of butter. *Slather* the butter on your bread.

Sip your drink, slowly, let the beverage linger in your mouth — interspersed with interesting, fascinating conversation. Sip, never ... slurp or gulp. Your glass should always be three-quarters full when his glass is empty.

Stay away from *ladies'* drinks: drinks like pink ladies, slow gin fizzes, daiquiris, gold cadillacs, Long Island iced teas, margaritas, piña coladas, mai tais, planters punch, white Russians, black Russians, red Russians, melon balls, blue balls, hummingbirds, hemorrhages and hurricanes. In short, avoid anything with sugar, or anything with an umbrella. Get your vitamin C from *fruit.* Don't order anything with Voodoo or Vixen in the title or sexual positions in the name like Dead Man Screw or the Missionary. *(She sort of titters.)*

Believe me, they are lethal ... I think you were conceived after one of those.

Drink, instead, like a man: straight up or on the rocks, with plenty of water in between.

Oh, yes. And never mix your drinks. Stay with one all night long, like the man you came in with: bourbon, gin, or tequila till dawn, damn the torpedoes, full speed ahead! *(As the Female*

18

Greek Chorus retreats, the Male Greek Chorus approaches the table as a Waiter.)

MALE GREEK CHORUS. *(As Waiter.)* I hope you all are having a pleasant evening. Is there something I can bring you, sir, before you order? *(Li'l Bit waits in anxious fear. Carefully, Uncle Peck says with command:)*

PECK. I'll have a plain iced tea. The lady would like a drink, I believe. *(The Male Greek Chorus does a double take; there is a moment when Uncle Peck and he are in silent communication.)*

MALE GREEK CHORUS. *(As Waiter.)* Very good. What would the ... lady like?

LI'L BIT. *(A bit flushed.)* Is there ... is there any sugar in a martini?

PECK. None that I know of.

LI'L BIT. That's what I'd like then — a dry martini. And could we maybe have some bread?

PECK. A drink fit for a woman of the world. — Please bring the lady a dry martini, be generous with the olives, straight up. *(The Male Greek Chorus anticipates a* large *tip.)*

MALE GREEK CHORUS. *(As Waiter.)* Right away. Very good, sir. *(The Male Greek Chorus returns with an empty martini glass which he puts in front of Li'l Bit.)*

PECK. Your glass is empty. Another martini, madam?

LI'L BIT. Yes, thank you. *(Peck signals the Male Greek Chorus, who nods.)* So why did you leave South Carolina, Uncle Peck?

PECK. I was stationed in D.C. after the war, and decided to stay. Go North, Young Man, someone might have said.

LI'L BIT. What did you do in the service anyway?

PECK. *(Suddenly taciturn.)* I ... I did just this and that. Nothing heroic or spectacular.

LI'L BIT. But did you see fighting? Or go to Europe?

PECK. I served in the Pacific Theater. It's really nothing interesting to talk about.

LI'L BIT. It is to me. *(The Waiter has brought another empty glass.)* Oh, goody. I love the color of the swizzle sticks. What were we talking about?

PECK. Swizzle sticks.

LI'L BIT. Do you ever think of going back?

19

PECK. To the Marines?

LI'L BIT. No — to South Carolina.

PECK. Well, we do go back. To visit.

LI'L BIT. No, I mean to live.

PECK. Not very likely. I think it's better if my mother doesn't have a daily reminder of her disappointment.

LI'L BIT. Are these floorboards slanted?

PECK. Yes, the floor is very slanted. I think this is the original floor.

LI'L BIT. Oh, good. *(The Female Greek Chorus as Mother enters swaying a little, a little past tipsy.)*

FEMALE GREEK CHORUS. *(As Mother.)* Don't leave your drink unattended when you visit the ladies' room. There is such a thing as white slavery; the modus operandi is to spike an unsuspecting young girl's drink with a "mickey" when she's left the room to powder her nose.

But if you feel you have had more than your sufficiency in liquor, do go to the ladies' room — often. Pop your head out of doors for a refreshing breath of the night air. If you must, wet your face and head with tap water. Don't be afraid to dunk your head if necessary. A wet woman is still less conspicuous than a drunk woman. *(The Female Greek Chorus stumbles a little; conspiratorially.)*

When in the course of human events it becomes necessary, go to a corner stall and insert the index and middle finger down the throat almost to the epiglottis. Divulge your stomach contents by such persuasion, and then wait a few moments before rejoining your beau waiting for you at your table.

Oh, no. Don't be shy or embarrassed. In the very best of establishments, there's always one or two debutantes crouched in the corner stalls, their beaded purses tossed willy-nilly, sounding like cats in heat, heaving up the contents of their stomachs. *(The Female Greek Chorus begins to wander off.)*

I wonder what it is they do in the men's rooms ...

LI'L BIT. So why is your mother disappointed in you, Uncle Peck?

PECK. Every mother in Horry County has Great Expectations.

LI'L BIT. — Could I have another mar-ti-ni, please?

PECK. I think this is your last one. *(Peck signals the Waiter. The Waiter looks at Li'l Bit and shakes his head no. Peck raises his eyebrow, raises his finger to indicate one more, and then rubs his fingers together. It looks like a secret code. The Waiter sighs, shakes his head sadly, and brings over another empty martini glass. He glares at Peck.)*

LI'L BIT. The name of the county where you grew up is "Horry?" *(Li'l Bit, plastered, begins to laugh. Then she stops.)* I think your mother should be proud of you. *(Peck signals for the check.)*

PECK. Well, missy, she wanted me to do — to *be* everything my father was not. She wanted me to amount to something.

LI'L BIT. But you have! You've amounted a lot ...

PECK. I'm just a very ordinary man. *(The Waiter has brought the check and waits. Peck draws out a large bill and hands it to the Waiter. Li'l Bit is in the soppy stage.)*

LI'L BIT. I'll bet your mother loves you, Uncle Peck. *(Peck freezes a bit. To Male Greek Chorus as Waiter:)*

PECK. Thank you. The service was exceptional. Please keep the change.

MALE GREEK CHORUS. *(As Waiter, in a tone that could freeze.)* Thank you, sir. Will you be needing any help?

PECK. I think we can manage, thank you. *(Just then, the Female Greek Chorus as Mother lurches on stage; the Male Greek Chorus as Waiter escorts her off as she delivers:)*

FEMALE GREEK CHORUS. *(As Mother.)* Thanks to judicious planning and several trips to the ladies' loo, your mother once out-drank an entire regiment of British officers on a good-will visit to Washington! Every last man of them! Milquetoasts! How'd they ever kick Hitler's cahones, huh? No match for an American lady — I could drink every man in here under the table. *(She delivers one last crucial hint before she is gently "bounced.")* As a last resort, when going out for an evening on the town, be sure to wear a skin-tight girdle — so tight that only a surgical knife or acetylene torch can get it off you — so that if you do pass out in the arms of your escort, he'll end up with rubber burns on his fingers before he can steal your virtue —

(A Voice punctuates the interlude with:)

Vehicle Failure.

Even with careful maintenance and preventive operation of your automobile, it is all too common for us to experience an unexpected breakdown. If you are driving at any speed when a breakdown occurs, you must slow down and guide the automobile to the side of the road.

(Peck is slowly propping up Li'l Bit as they work their way to his car in the parking lot of the inn.)

PECK.   How are you doing, missy?

LI'L BIT.   It's so far to the car, Uncle Peck. Like the lanterns in the trees the British fired on ... *(Li'l Bit stumbles. Peck swoops her up in his arms.)*

PECK.   Okay. I think we're going to take a more direct route. *(Li'l Bit closes her eyes.)* Dizzy? *(She nods her head.)* Don't look at the ground. Almost there — do you feel sick to your stomach? *(Li'l Bit nods. They reach the "car." Peck gently deposits her on the front seat.)* Just settle here a little while until things stop spinning. *(Li'l Bit opens her eyes.)*

LI'L BIT.   What are we doing?

PECK.   We're just going to sit here until your tummy settles down.

LI'L BIT.   It's such nice upholst'ry —

PECK.   Think you can go for a ride, now?

LI'L BIT.   Where are you taking me?

PECK.   Home.

LI'L BIT.   You're not taking me — upstairs? There's no room at the inn? *(Li'l Bit giggles.)*

PECK.   Do you want to go upstairs? *(Li'l Bit doesn't answer.)* Or home?

LI'L BIT.   — This isn't right, Uncle Peck.

PECK.   What isn't right?

LI'L BIT.   What we're doing. It's wrong. It's very wrong.

PECK.   What are we doing? *(Li'l Bit does not answer.)* We're just going out to dinner.

LI'L BIT.   You know. It's not nice to Aunt Mary.

PECK.   You let me be the judge of what's nice and not nice to my wife. *(Beat.)*

LI'L BIT.   Now you're mad.

22

PECK. I'm not mad. It's just that I thought you ... understood me, Li'l Bit. I think you're the only one who does.

LI'L BIT. Someone will get hurt.

PECK. Have I forced you to do anything? *(There is a long pause as Li'l Bit tries to get sober enough to think this through.)*

LI'L BIT. ... I guess not.

PECK. We are just enjoying each other's company. I've told you, nothing is going to happen between us until you want it to. Do you know that?

LI'L BIT. Yes.

PECK. Nothing is going to happen until you want it to. *(A second more, with Peck staring ahead at the river while seated at the wheel of his car. Then, softly:)* Do you want something to happen? *(Peck reaches over and strokes her face, very gently. Li'l Bit softens, reaches for him, and buries her head in his neck. Then she kisses him. Then she moves away, dizzy again.)*

LI'L BIT. ... I don't know. *(Peck smiles; this has been good news for him — it hasn't been a "no.")*

PECK. Then I'll wait. I'm a very patient man. I've been waiting for a long time. I don't mind waiting.

LI'L BIT. Someone is going to get hurt.

PECK. No one is going to get hurt. *(Li'l Bit closes her eyes.)* Are you feeling sick?

LI'L BIT. Sleepy. *(Carefully, Peck props Li'l Bit up on the seat.)*

PECK. Stay here a second.

LI'L BIT. Where're you going?

PECK. I'm getting something from the back seat.

LI'L BIT. *(Scared; too loud.)* What? What are you going to do? *(Peck reappears in the front seat with a lap rug.)*

PECK. Shhhh. *(Peck covers Li'l Bit. She calms down.)* There. Think you can sleep? *(Li'l Bit nods. She slides over to rest on his shoulder. With a look of happiness, Peck turns the ignition key. Beat. Peck leaves Li'l Bit sleeping in the car and strolls down to the audience. Wagner's* Flying Dutchman * comes up faintly.*

A Voice interjects:)

Idling in the Neutral Gear.

TEENAGE GREEK CHORUS.   Uncle Peck Teaches Cousin
Bobby How to Fish.

PECK.   I get back once or twice a year — supposedly to visit
Mama and the family, but the real truth is to fish. I miss this
the most of all. There's a smell in the Low Country — where
the swamp and fresh inlet join the saltwater — a scent of sand
and cypress, that I haven't found anywhere yet.

I don't say this very often up North because it will just play
into the stereotype everyone has, but I will tell you: I didn't wear
shoes in the summertime until I was sixteen. It's unnatural
down here to pen up your feet in leather. Go ahead — take 'em
off. Let yourself breathe — it really will make you feel better.

We're going to aim for some pompano today — and I have
to tell you, they're a very shy, mercurial fish. Takes patience,
and psychology. You have to believe it doesn't matter if you
catch one or not.

Sky's pretty spectacular — there's some beer in the cooler
next to the crab salad I packed, so help yourself if you get hungry. Are you hungry? Thirsty? Holler if you are.

Okay. You don't want to lean over the bridge like that —
pompano feed in shallow water, and you don't want to get too
close — they're frisky and shy little things — wait, check your
line. Yep, something's been munching while we were talking.

Okay, look: We take the sand flea and you take the hook
like this — right through his little sand flea rump. Sand fleas
should always keep their backs to the wall. Okay. Cast it in, like
I showed you. That's great! I can taste that pompano now,
sautéed with some pecans and butter, a little bourbon — now
— let it lie on the bottom — now, reel, jerk, reel, jerk —

Look — look at your line. There's something calling, all
right. Okay, tip the rod up — not too sharp — hook it — all
right, now easy, reel and then rest — let it play. And reel —
play it out, that's right — really good! I can't believe it! It's a
pompano. — Good work! Way to go! You are an official fish-
erman now. Pompano are hard to catch. We are going to have
a delicious little —

* See Special Note on Songs and Recordings on copyright page.

24

What? Well, I don't know how much pain a fish feels — you can't think of that. Oh, no, don't cry, come on now, it's just a fish — the other guys are going to see you. — No, no, you're just real sensitive, and I think that's wonderful at your age — look, do you want me to cut it free? You do?

Okay, hand me those pliers — look — I'm cutting the hook — okay? And we're just going to drop it in — no I'm not mad. It's just for fun, okay? There — it's going to swim back to its lady friend and tell her what a terrible day it had and she's going to stroke him with her fins until he feels better, and then they'll do something alone together that will make them both feel good and sleepy ...

(Peck bends down, very earnest.) I don't want you to feel ashamed about crying. I'm not going to tell anyone, okay? I can keep secrets. You know, men cry all the time. They just don't tell anybody, and they don't let anybody catch them. There's nothing you could do that would make me feel ashamed of you. Do you know that? Okay. *(Peck straightens up, smiles.)*

Do you want to pack up and call it a day? I tell you what — I think I can still remember — there's a really neat tree house where I used to stay for days. I think it's still here — it was the last time I looked. But it's a secret place — you can't tell anybody we've gone there — least of all your mom or your sisters. — This is something special just between you and me. Sound good? We'll climb up there and have a beer and some crab salad — okay, B.B.? Bobby? Robert ... *(Li'l Bit sits at a kitchen table with the two Female Greek Chorus members.)*

LI'L BIT. *(To the audience.)* Three women, three generations, sit at the kitchen table.

On Men, Sex, and Women: Part I:

FEMALE GREEK CHORUS. *(As Mother.)* Men only want one thing.

LI'L BIT. *(Wide-eyed.)* But what? What is it they want?

FEMALE GREEK CHORUS. *(As Mother.)* And once they have it, they lose all interest. So Don't Give It to Them.

TEENAGE GREEK CHORUS. *(As Grandmother.)* I never had the luxury of the rhythm method. Your grandfather is just a big bull. A big bull. Every morning, every evening.

25

FEMALE GREEK CHORUS. *(As Mother, whispers to Li'l Bit.)* And he used to come home for lunch every day.

LI'L BIT. My god, Grandma!

TEENAGE GREEK CHORUS. *(As Grandmother.)* Your grandfather only cares that I do two things: have the table set and the bed turned down.

FEMALE GREEK CHORUS. *(As Mother.)* And in all that time, Mother, you never have experienced — ?

LI'L BIT. *(To the audience.)* — Now my grandmother believed in all the sacraments of the church, to the day she died. She believed in Santa Claus and the Easter Bunny until she was fifteen. But she didn't believe in —

TEENAGE GREEK CHORUS. *(As Grandmother.)* — Orgasm! That's just something you and Mary have made up! I don't believe you.

FEMALE GREEK CHORUS. *(As Mother.)* Mother, it happens to women all the time —

TEENAGE GREEK CHORUS. *(As Grandmother.)* — Oh, now you're going to tell me about the G force!

LI'L BIT. No, Grandma, I think that's astronauts —

FEMALE GREEK CHORUS. *(As Mother.)* Well, Mama, after all, you were a child bride when Big Papa came and got you — you were a married woman and you still believed in Santa Claus.

TEENAGE GREEK CHORUS. *(As Grandmother.)* It was legal, what Daddy and I did! I was fourteen and in those days, fourteen was a grown-up woman — *(Big Papa shuffles in the kitchen for a cookie.)*

MALE GREEK CHORUS. *(As Grandfather.)* — Oh, now we're off on Grandma and the Rape of the Sa-bean Women!

TEENAGE GREEK CHORUS. *(As Grandmother.)* Well, you were the one in such a big hurry —

MALE GREEK CHORUS. *(As Grandfather to Li'l Bit.)* — I picked your grandmother out of that herd of sisters just like a lion chooses the gazelle — the plump, slow, flaky gazelle dawdling at the edge of the herd — your sisters were too smart and too fast and too scrawny —

LI'L BIT. *(To the audience.)* — The family story is that when Big Papa came for Grandma, my Aunt Lily was waiting for him with

26

a broom — and she beat him over the head all the way down the stairs as he was carrying out Grandma's hope chest —

MALE GREEK CHORUS. *(As Grandfather.)* — And they were *mean.* 'Specially Lily.

FEMALE GREEK CHORUS. *(As Mother.)* Well, you were robbing the baby of the family!

TEENAGE GREEK CHORUS. *(As Grandmother.)* I still keep a broom handy in the kitchen! And I know how to use it! So get your hand out of the cookie jar and don't you spoil your appetite for dinner — out of the kitchen! *(Male Greek Chorus as Grandfather leaves chuckling with a cookie.)*

FEMALE GREEK CHORUS. *(As Mother.)* Just one thing a married woman needs to know how to use — the rolling pin or the broom. I prefer a heavy, cast-iron fry pan — they're great on a man's head, no matter how thick the skull is.

TEENAGE GREEK CHORUS. *(As Grandmother.)* Yes, sir, your father is ruled by only two bosses! Mr. Gut and Mr. Peter! And sometimes, first thing in the morning, Mr. Sphincter Muscle!

FEMALE GREEK CHORUS. *(As Mother.)* It's true. Men are like children. Just like little boys.

TEENAGE GREEK CHORUS. *(As Grandmother.)* Men are bulls! Big bulls! *(The Greek Chorus is getting aroused.)*

FEMALE GREEK CHORUS. *(As Mother.)* They'd still be crouched on their haunches over a fire in a cave if we hadn't cleaned them up!

TEENAGE GREEK CHORUS. *(As Grandmother, flushed.)* Coming in smelling of sweat —

FEMALE GREEK CHORUS. *(As Mother.)* — Looking at those naughty pictures like boys in a dime store with a dollar in their pockets!

TEENAGE GREEK CHORUS. *(As Grandmother; raucous.)* No matter to them what they smell like! They've got to have it, right then, on the spot, right there! Nasty! —

FEMALE GREEK CHORUS. *(As Mother.)* — Vulgar!

TEENAGE GREEK CHORUS. *(As Grandmother.)* Primitive! —

FEMALE GREEK CHORUS. *(As Mother.)* — Hot! —

LI'L BIT. And just about then, Big Papa would shuffle in with —

MALE GREEK CHORUS. *(As Grandfather.)* — What are you all cackling about in here?

TEENAGE GREEK CHORUS. *(As Grandmother.)* Stay out of the kitchen! This is just for girls! *(As Grandfather leaves:)*

MALE GREEK CHORUS. *(As Grandfather.)* Lucy, you'd better not be filling Mama's head with sex! Every time you and Mary come over and start in about sex, when I ask a simple question like, "What time is dinner going to be ready?," Mama snaps my head off!

TEENAGE GREEK CHORUS. *(As Grandmother.)* Dinner will be ready when I'm good and ready! Stay out of this kitchen! *(Li'l Bit steps out.*

A Voice directs:)

When Making a Left Turn, You Must Downshift While Going Forward.

LI'L BIT. 1979. A long bus trip to Upstate New York. I settled in to read, when a young man sat beside me.

MALE GREEK CHORUS. *(As Young Man; voice cracking.)* "What are you reading?"

LI'L BIT. He asked. His voice broke into that miserable equivalent of vocal acne, not quite falsetto and not tenor, either. I glanced a side view. He was appealing in an odd way, huge ears at a defiant angle springing forward at ninety degrees. He must have been shaving, because his face, with a peach sheen, was speckled with nicks and styptic. "I have a class tomorrow," I told him.

MALE GREEK CHORUS. *(As Young Man.)* "You're taking a class?"

LI'L BIT. "I'm teaching a class." He concentrated on lowering his voice.

MALE GREEK CHORUS. *(As Young Man.)* "I'm a senior. Walt Whitman High."

LI'L BIT. The light was fading outside, so perhaps he was — with a very high voice.

I felt his "interest" quicken. Five steps ahead of the hopes in his head, I slowed down, waited, pretended surprise, acted at listening, all the while knowing we would get off the bus, he would just then seem to think to ask me to dinner, he would chivalrously insist on walking me home, he would continue to converse in the street until I would casually invite him up to my room — and — I was only into the second moment of conversation and I could see the whole evening before me.

And dramaturgically speaking, after the faltering and slightly comical "first act," there was the very briefest of intermissions, and an extremely capable and forceful and *sustained* second act. And after the second act climax and a gentle denouement — before the post-play discussion — I lay on my back in the dark and I thought about you, Uncle Peck. Oh. Oh — this is the allure. Being older. Being the first. Being the translator, the teacher, the epicure, the already jaded. This is how the giver gets taken.

(Li'l Bit changes her tone.) On Men, Sex, and Women: Part II: *(Li'l Bit steps back into the scene as a fifteen year old, gawky and quiet, as the gazelle at the edge of the herd.)*

TEENAGE GREEK CHORUS. *(As Grandmother; to Li'l Bit.)* You're being mighty quiet, missy. Cat Got Your Tongue?

LI'L BIT. I'm just listening. Just thinking.

TEENAGE GREEK CHORUS. *(As Grandmother.)* Oh, yes, Little Miss Radar Ears? Soaking it all in? Little Miss Sponge? Penny for your thoughts? *(Li'l Bit hesitates to ask but she really wants to know.)*

LI'L BIT. Does it — when you do it — you know, theoretically when I do it and I haven't done it before — I mean — does it hurt?

FEMALE GREEK CHORUS. *(As Mother.)* Does what hurt, honey?

LI'L BIT. When a … when a girl does it for the first time — with a man — does it hurt?

TEENAGE GREEK CHORUS. *(As Grandmother; horrified.)* That's what you're thinking about?

FEMALE GREEK CHORUS. *(As Mother; calm.)* Well, just a little bit. Like a pinch. And there's a little blood.

TEENAGE GREEK CHORUS. *(As Grandmother.)* Don't tell her that! She's too young to be thinking those things!

FEMALE GREEK CHORUS. *(As Mother.)* Well, if she doesn't find out from me, where is she going to find out? In the street?

TEENAGE GREEK CHORUS. *(As Grandmother.)* Tell her it hurts! It's agony! You think you're going to die! Especially if you do it before marriage!

FEMALE GREEK CHORUS. *(As Mother.)* Mama! I'm going to tell her the truth! Unlike you, you left me and Mary completely in the dark with fairy tales and told us to go to the priest! What does an eighty-year-old priest know about love-making with girls!

LI'L BIT. *(Getting upset.)* It's not fair!

FEMALE GREEK CHORUS. *(As Mother.)* Now, see, she's getting upset — you're scaring her.

TEENAGE GREEK CHORUS. *(As Grandmother.)* Good! Let her be good and scared! It hurts! You bleed like a stuck pig! And you lay there and say, "Why, O Lord, have you forsaken me?!"

LI'L BIT. It's not fair! Why does everything have to hurt for girls? Why is there always blood?

FEMALE GREEK CHORUS. *(As Mother.)* It's not a lot of blood — and it feels wonderful after the pain subsides …

TEENAGE GREEK CHORUS. *(As Grandmother.)* You're encouraging her to just go out and find out with the first drugstore joe who buys her a milk shake!

FEMALE GREEK CHORUS. *(As Mother.)* Don't be scared. It won't hurt you — if the man you go to bed with really loves you. It's important that he loves you.

TEENAGE GREEK CHORUS. *(As Grandmother.)* — Why don't you just go out and rent a motel room for her, Lucy?

FEMALE GREEK CHORUS. *(As Mother.)* I believe in telling my daughter the truth! We have a very close relationship! I want her to be able to ask me anything — I'm not scaring her with stories about Eve's sin and snakes crawling on their bellies for eternity and women bearing children in mortal pain —

TEENAGE GREEK CHORUS. *(As Grandmother.)* — If she stops and thinks before she takes her knickers off, maybe someone in this family will finish high school! *(Li'l Bit knows what is about to happen and starts to retreat from the scene at this point.)*

FEMALE GREEK CHORUS. *(As Mother.)* Mother! If you and Daddy had helped me — I wouldn't have had to marry that — that no-good-son-of-a —

TEENAGE GREEK CHORUS.   *(As Grandmother.)* — He was good enough for you on a full moon! I hold you responsible!
FEMALE GREEK CHORUS.   *(As Mother.)* — You could have helped me! You could have told me something about the facts of life!
TEENAGE GREEK CHORUS.   *(As Grandmother.)* — I told you what my mother told me! A girl with her skirt up can outrun a man with his pants down! *(The Male Greek Chorus enters the fray; L'il Bit edges further D.)*
FEMALE GREEK CHORUS.   *(As Mother.)* And when I turned to you for a little help, all I got afterwards was —
MALE GREEK CHORUS.   *(As Grandfather.)* You Made Your Bed; Now Lie On It! *(The Greek Chorus freezes, mouths open, argumentatively.)*
LI'L BIT.   *(To the audience.)* Oh, please! I still can't bear to listen to it, after all these years — *(The Male Greek Chorus "unfreezes," but out of his open mouth, as if to his surprise, comes a base refrain from a Motown* song.)*
MALE GREEK CHORUS.   "Do-Bee-Do-Wah!" *(The Female Greek Chorus member is also surprised; but she, too, unfreezes.)*
FEMALE GREEK CHORUS.   "Shoo-doo-be-doo-be-doo; shoo-doo-be-doo-be-doo." *(The Male and Female Greek Chorus members continue with their harmony, until the Teenage member of the Chorus starts in with Motown lyrics such as "Dedicated to the One I Love,"* or "In the Still of the Night,"* or "Hold Me"* — any Sam Cooke will do. The three modulate down into three part harmony, softly, until they are submerged by the actual recording playing over the radio in the car in which Uncle Peck sits in the driver's seat, waiting. Li'l Bit sits in the passenger's seat.)*
LI'L BIT.   Ahh. That's better. *(Uncle Peck reaches over and turns the volume down; to Li'l Bit.)*
PECK.   How can you hear yourself think? *(Li'l Bit does not answer.*

A Voice insinuates itself in the pause:)
Before You Drive.

---

* See Special Note on Songs and Recordings on copyright page.

Always check under your car for obstructions — broken bottles, fallen tree branches, and the bodies of small children. Each year hundreds of children are crushed beneath the wheels of unwary drivers in their own driveways. Children depend on *you* to watch them.

(Pause. The Voice continues.)

You and the Reverse Gear.

(In the following section, it would be nice to have slides of erotic photographs of women and cars: women posed over the hood; women draped along the sideboards; women with water hoses spraying the car; and the actress playing Li'l Bit with a Bel Air or any 1950s car one can find for the finale.)

LI'L BIT. 1967. In a parking lot of the Beltsville Agricultural Farms. The Initiation into a Boy's First Love.

PECK. *(With a soft look on his face.)* Of course, my favorite car will always be the '56 Bel Air Sports Coupe. Chevy sold more '55s, but the '56! — a V-8 with Corvette option, 225 horsepower; went from zero to sixty miles per hour in 8.9 seconds.

LI'L BIT. *(To the audience.)* Long after a mother's tits, but before a woman's breasts:

PECK. Super-Turbo-Fire! What a Power Pack — mechanical lifters, twin four-barrel carbs, lightweight valves, dual exhausts —

LI'L BIT. *(To the audience.)* After the milk but before the beer:

PECK. A specific intake manifold, higher-lift camshaft, and the tightest squeeze Chevy had ever made —

LI'L BIT. *(To the audience.)* Long after he's squeezed down the birth canal but before he's pushed his way back in: The boy falls in love with the thing that bears his weight with speed.

PECK. I want you to know your automobile inside and out. — Are you there? Li'l Bit? *(Slides end here.)*

LI'L BIT. — What?

PECK. You're drifting. I need you to concentrate.

LI'L BIT. Sorry.

PECK. Okay. Get into the driver's seat. *(Li'l Bit does.)* Okay. Now. Show me what you're going to do before you start the car. *(Li'l Bit sits, with her hands in her lap. She starts to giggle.)*

LI'L BIT. I don't know, Uncle Peck.

PECK.   Now, come on. What's the first thing you're going to adjust?

LI'L BIT.   My bra strap? —

PECK.   — Li'l Bit. What's the most important thing to have control of on the inside of the car?

LI'L BIT.   That's easy. The radio. I tune the radio from Mama's old fart tunes to — *(Li'l Bit turns the radio up so we can hear a 1960s tune.* With surprising firmness, Peck commands.)*

PECK.   — Radio off. Right now. *(Li'l Bit turns the radio off.)* When you are driving your car, with your license, you can fiddle with the stations all you want. But when you are driving with a learner's permit in my car, I want all your attention to be on the road.

LI'L BIT.   Yes, sir.

PECK.   Okay. Now the seat — forward and up. *(Li'l Bit pushes it forward.)* Do you want a cushion?

LI'L BIT.   No — I'm good.

PECK.   You should be able to reach all the switches and controls. Your feet should be able to push the accelerator, brake and clutch all the way down. Can you do that?

LI'L BIT.   Yes.

PECK.   Okay, the side mirrors. You want to be able to see just a bit of the right side of the car in the right mirror — can you?

LI'L BIT.   Turn it out more.

PECK.   Okay. How's that?

LI'L BIT.   A little more … Okay, that's good.

PECK.   Now the left — again, you want to be able to see behind you — but the left lane — adjust it until you feel comfortable. *(Li'l Bit does so.)* Next. I want you to check the rearview mirror. Angle it so you have a clear vision of the back. *(Li'l Bit does so.)* Okay. Lock your door. Make sure all the doors are locked.

LI'L BIT.   *(Making a joke of it.)* But then I'm locked in with you.

PECK.   Don't fool.

LI'L BIT.   All right. We're locked in.

PECK.   We'll deal with the air vents and defroster later. I'm

* See Special Note on Songs and Recordings on copyright page.

teaching you on a manual — once you learn manual, you can drive anything. I want you to be able to drive any car, any machine. Manual gives you *control*. In ice, if your brakes fail, if you need more power — okay? It's a little harder at first, but then it becomes like breathing. Now. Put your hands on the wheel. I never want to see you driving with one hand. Always two hands. *(Li'l Bit hesitates.)* What? What is it now?

LI'L BIT.   If I put my hands on the wheel — how do I defend myself?

PECK.   *(Softly.)* Now listen. Listen up close. We're not going to fool around with this. This is serious business. I will never touch you when you are driving a car. Understand?

LI'L BIT.   Okay.

PECK.   Hands on the nine o'clock and three o'clock position gives you maximum control and turn. *(Peck goes silent for a while. Li'l Bit waits for more instruction.)*

Okay. Just relax and listen to me, Li'l Bit, okay? I want you to lift your hands for a second and look at them. *(Li'l Bit feels a bit silly, but does it.)*

Those are your two hands. When you are driving, your life is in your own two hands. Understand? *(Li'l Bit nods.)*

I don't have any sons. You're the nearest to a son I'll ever have — and I want to give you something. Something that really matters to me.

There's something about driving — when you're in control of the car, just you and the machine and the road — that nobody can take from you. A power. I feel more myself in my car than anywhere else. And that's what I want to give to you.

There's a lot of assholes out there. Crazy men, arrogant idiots, drunks, angry kids, geezers who are blind — and you have to be ready for them. I want to teach you to drive like a man.

LI'L BIT.   What does that mean?

PECK.   Men are taught to drive with confidence — with aggression. The road belongs to them. They drive defensively — always looking out for the other guy. Women tend to be polite — to hesitate. And that can be fatal.

You're going to learn to think what the other guy is going to do before he does it. If there's an accident, and ten cars pile

34

up, and people get killed, you're the one who's gonna steer through it, put your foot on the gas if you have to, and be the only one to walk away. I don't know how long you or I are going to live, but we're for damned sure not going to die in a car.

So if you're going to drive with me, I want you to take this very seriously.

LI'L BIT.   I will, Uncle Peck. I want you to teach me to drive.

PECK.   Good. You're going to pass your test on the first try. Perfect score. Before the next four weeks are over, you're going to know this baby inside and out. Treat her with respect.

LI'L BIT.   Why is it a "she?"

PECK.   Good question. It doesn't have to be a "she" — but when you close your eyes and think of someone who responds to your touch — someone who performs just for you and gives you what you ask for — I guess I always see a "she." You can call her what you like.

LI'L BIT.   *(To the audience.)* I closed my eyes — and decided not to change the gender.

(A Voice:)

Defensive driving involves defending yourself from hazardous and sudden changes in your automotive environment. By thinking ahead, the defensive driver can adjust to weather, road conditions and road kill. Good defensive driving involves mental and physical preparation. Are you prepared?

(Another Voice chimes in:)

You and the Reverse Gear.

LI'L BIT.   1966. The Anthropology of the Female Body in Ninth Grade — Or A Walk Down Mammary Lane. *(Throughout the following, there is occasional rhythmic beeping, like a transmitter signalling. Li'l Bit is aware of it, but can't figure out where it is coming from. No one else seems to hear it.)*

MALE GREEK CHORUS.   In the hallway of Francis Scott Key Middle School. *(A bell rings; the Greek Chorus is changing classes and meets in the hall, conspiratorially.)*

TEENAGE GREEK CHORUS.   She's coming! *(Li'l Bit enters the scene; the Male Greek Chorus member has a sudden, violent sneezing and lethal allergy attack.)*

FEMALE GREEK CHORUS.   Jerome? Jerome? Are you all right?

MALE GREEK CHORUS.   I — don't — know. I can't breathe — get Li'l Bit —

TEENAGE GREEK CHORUS.   — He needs oxygen! —

FEMALE GREEK CHORUS.   — Can you help us here?

LI'L BIT.   What's wrong? Do you want me to get the school nurse — *(The Male Greek Chorus member wheezes, grabs his throat and sniffs at Li'l Bit's chest, which is beeping away.)*

MALE GREEK CHORUS.   No — it's okay — I only get this way when I'm around an allergy trigger —

LI'L BIT.   Golly. What are you allergic to?

MALE GREEK CHORUS.   *(With a sudden grab of her breast.)* Foam rubber. *(The Greek Chorus members break up with hilarity; Jerome leaps away from Li'l Bit's kicking rage with agility; as he retreats:)*

LI'L BIT.   Jerome! Creep! Cretin! Cro-Magnon!

TEENAGE GREEK CHORUS.   Rage is not attractive in a girl.

FEMALE GREEK CHORUS.   Really. Get a Sense of Humor.

(A Voice echoes:)

Good defensive driving involves mental and physical preparation. Were You Prepared?

FEMALE GREEK CHORUS.   Gym Class: In the showers. *(The sudden sound of water; the Female Greek Chorus members and Li'l Bit, while fully clothed, drape towels across their fronts, miming nudity. They stand, hesitate, at an imaginary shower's edge.)*

LI'L BIT.   Water looks hot.

FEMALE GREEK CHORUS.   Yesss … *(Female Greek Chorus members are not going to make the first move. One dips a tentative toe under the water, clutching the towel around her.)*

LI'L BIT.   Well, I guess we'd better shower and get out of here.

FEMALE GREEK CHORUS.   Yep. You go ahead. I'm still cooling off.

LI'L BIT.   Okay. — Sally? Are you gonna shower?

TEENAGE GREEK CHORUS.   After you — *(Li'l Bit takes a deep breath for courage, drops the towel and plunges in: The two Female Greek Chorus members look at Li'l Bit in the all together, laugh, gasp and high-five each other.)* Oh my god! Can you believe —

FEMALE GREEK CHORUS.   Told you! It's not foam rubber! I win! Jerome owes me fifty cents!

(A Voice editorializes:)

Were You Prepared?

(Li'l Bit tries to cover up; she is exposed, as suddenly 1960s Motown* fills the room and we segue into:)

FEMALE GREEK CHORUS.   The Sock Hop. *(Li'l Bit stands up against the wall with her female classmates. Teenage Greek Chorus is mesmerized by the music and just sways alone, lip-synching the lyrics.)*

LI'L BIT.   I don't know. Maybe it's just me — but — do you ever feel like you're just a walking Mary Jane joke?

FEMALE GREEK CHORUS.   I don't know what you mean.

LI'L BIT.   You haven't heard the Mary Jane jokes? *(Female Greek Chorus member shakes her head no.)* Okay. "Little Mary Jane is walking through the woods, when all of a sudden this man who was hiding behind a tree *jumps* out, *rips* open Mary Jane's blouse, and *plunges* his hands on her breasts. And Little Mary Jane just laughed and laughed because she knew her money was in her shoes." *(Li'l Bit laughs; the Female Greek Chorus does not.)*

FEMALE GREEK CHORUS.   You're weird. *(In another space, in a strange light, Uncle Peck stands and stares at Li'l Bit's body. He is setting up a tripod, but he just stands, appreciative, watching her.)*

LI'L BIT.   Well, don't you ever feel ... self-conscious? Like you're being looked at all the time?

FEMALE GREEK CHORUS.   That's not a problem for me. — Oh — look — Greg's coming over to ask you to dance. *(Teenage Greek Chorus becomes attentive, flustered. Male Greek Chorus member, as Greg, bends slightly as a very short young man, whose head is at Li'l Bit's chest level. Ardent, sincere and socially inept, Greg will become a successful gynecologist.)*

TEENAGE GREEK CHORUS.   *(Softly.)* Hi, Greg. *(Greg does not hear. He is intent on only one thing.)*

MALE GREEK CHORUS.   *(As Greg, to Li'l Bit.)* Good Evening. Would you care to dance?

LI'L BIT.   *(Gently.)* Thank you very much, Greg — but I'm going to sit this one out.

MALE GREEK CHORUS.   *(As Greg.)* Oh. Okay. I'll try my luck later. *(He disappears.)*

* See Special Note on Songs and Recordings on copyright page.

TEENAGE GREEK CHORUS.   Oohhh. *(Li'l Bit relaxes. Then she tenses, aware of Peck's gaze.)*
FEMALE GREEK CHORUS.   Take pity on him. Someone should.
LI'L BIT.   But he's so short.
TEENAGE GREEK CHORUS.   He can't help it.
LI'L BIT.   But his head comes up to *(Li'l Bit gestures.)* here. And I think he asks me on the fast dances so he can watch me — you know — jiggle.
FEMALE GREEK CHORUS.   I wish I had your problems. *(The tune changes; Greg is across the room in a flash.)*
MALE GREEK CHORUS.   *(As Greg.)* Evening again. May I ask you for the honor of a spin on the floor?
LI'L BIT.   I'm ... very complimented, Greg. But I ... I just don't do fast dances.
MALE GREEK CHORUS.   *(As Greg.)* Oh. No problem. That's okay. *(He disappears. Teenage Greek Chorus watches him go.)*
TEENAGE GREEK CHORUS.   That is just so — sad. *(Li'l Bit becomes aware of Peck waiting.)*
FEMALE GREEK CHORUS.   You know, you should take it as a compliment that the guys want to watch you jiggle. They're guys. That's what they're supposed to do.
LI'L BIT.   I guess you're right. But sometimes I feel like these alien life forces, these two mounds of flesh have grafted themselves onto my chest, and they're using me until they can "propagate" and take over the world and they'll just keep growing, with a mind of their own until I collapse under their weight and they suck all the nourishment out of my body and I finally just waste away while they get bigger and bigger and — *(Li'l Bit's classmates are just staring at her in disbelief.)*
FEMALE GREEK CHORUS.   — You are the strangest girl I have ever met. *(Li'l Bit's trying to joke but feels on the verge of tears.)*
LI'L BIT.   Or maybe someone's implanted radio transmitters in my chest at a frequency I can't hear, that girls can't detect, but they're sending out these signals to men who get mesmerized, like sirens, calling them to dash themselves on these "rocks" — *(Just then, the music segues into a slow dance, perhaps a Beach Boys tune like "Little Surfer,"* but over the music there's a rhyth-*

38

mic, hypnotic beeping transmitted, which both Greg and Peck hear. Li'l Bit hears it too, and in horror she stares at her chest. She, too, is almost hypnotized. In a trance, Greg responds to the signals and is called to her side — actually, her front. Like a zombie, he stands in front of her, his eyes planted on her two orbs.)

MALE GREEK CHORUS. *(As Greg.)* This one's a slow dance. I hope your dance card isn't … filled? *(Li'l Bit is aware of Peck; but the signals are calling her to him. The signals are no longer transmitters, but an electromagnetic force, pulling Li'l Bit to his side, where he again waits for her to join him. She must get away from the dance floor.)*

LI'L BIT.   Greg — you really are a nice boy. But I don't like to dance.

MALE GREEK CHORUS.   *(As Greg.)* That's okay. We don't have to move or anything. I could just hold you and we could just *sway* a little —

LI'L BIT.   — No! I'm sorry — but I think I have to leave; I hear someone calling me — *(Li'l Bit starts across the dance floor, leaving Greg behind. The beeping stops. The lights change, although the music does not. As Li'l Bit talks to the audience, she continues to change and prepare for the coming session. She should be wearing a tight tank top or a sheer blouse and very tight pants. To the audience.)*

In every man's home some small room, some zone in his house, is set aside. It might be the attic, or the study, or a den. And there's an invisible sign as if from the old treehouse: Girls Keep Out.

Here, away from female eyes, lace doilies and crochet, he keeps his manly toys: the Vargas pinups, the tackle. A scent of tobacco and WD-40. *(She inhales deeply.)* A dash of his Bay Rum. Ahhh … *(Li'l Bit savors it for just a moment more.)*

Here he keeps his secrets: a violin or saxophone, drum set or darkroom, and the stacks of *Playboy. (In a whisper.)* Here, in my aunt's home, it was the basement. Uncle Peck's turf.

(A Voice commands:)

You and the Reverse Gear.

LI'L BIT.   1965. The Photo Shoot. *(Li'l Bit steps into the scene as a nervous but curious thirteen year old. Music, from the previous scene, continues to play, changing into something like Roy Orbison* later — something seductive with a beat. Peck fiddles, all business, with his camera. As in the driving lesson, he is all competency and concentration. Li'l Bit stands awkwardly. He looks through the Leica camera on the tripod, adjusts the back lighting, etc.)*

PECK.   Are you cold? The lights should heat up some in a few minutes —

LI'L BIT.   — Aunt Mary is?

PECK.   At the National Theatre matinee. With your mother. We have time.

LI'L BIT.   But — what if —

PECK.   — And so what if they return? I told them you and I were going to be working with my camera. They won't come down. *(Li'l Bit is quiet, apprehensive.)* — Look, are you sure you want to do this?

LI'L BIT.   I said I'd do it. But —

PECK.   — I know. You've drawn the line.

LI'L BIT.   *(Reassured.)* That's right. No frontal nudity.

PECK.   Good heavens, girl, where did you pick that up?

LI'L BIT.   *(Defensive.)* I *read. (Peck tries not to laugh.)*

PECK.   And I read *Playboy* for the interviews. Okay. Let's try some different music. *(Peck goes to an expensive reel-to-reel and forwards. Something like "Sweet Dreams"* begins to play.)*

LI'L BIT.   I didn't know you listened to this.

PECK.   I'm not dead, you know. I try to keep up. Do you like this song? *(Li'l Bit nods with pleasure.)* Good. Now listen — at professional photo shoots, they always play music for the models. Okay? I want you to just enjoy the music. Listen to it with your body, and just — respond.

LI'L BIT.   Respond to the music with my ... body?

PECK.   Right. Almost like dancing. Here — let's get you on the stool, first. *(Peck comes over and helps her up.)*

LI'L BIT.   But nothing showing — *(Peck firmly, with his large*

---

* See Special Note on Songs and Recordings on copyright page.

capable hands, brushes back her hair, angles her face. Li'l Bit turns to him like a plant to the sun.)

PECK.   Nothing showing. Just a peek. *(He holds her by the shoulder, looking at her critically. Then he unbuttons her blouse to the midpoint, and runs his hands over the flesh of her exposed sternum, arranging the fabric, just touching her. Deliberately, calmly. Asexually. Li'l Bit quiets, sits perfectly still, and closes her eyes.)* Okay?

LI'L BIT.   Yes. *(Peck goes back to his camera.)*

PECK.   I'm going to keep talking to you. Listen without responding to what I'm saying; you want to *listen* to the music. Sway, move just your torso or your head — I've got to check the light meter.

LI'L BIT.   But — you'll be watching.

PECK.   No — I'm not here — just my voice. Pretend you're in your room all alone on a Friday night with your mirror — and the music feels good — just move for me, Li'l Bit — *(Li'l Bit closes her eyes. At first self-conscious; then she gets more into the music and begins to sway. We hear the camera start to whir. Throughout the shoot, there can be a slide montage of actual shots of the actor playing Li'l Bit — interspersed with other models à la* Playboy, *Calvin Klein and Victoriana/Lewis Carroll's Alice Liddell.)*

That's it. That looks great. Okay. Just keep doing that. Lift your head up a bit more, good, good, just keep moving, that a girl — you're a very beautiful young woman. Do you know that? *(Li'l Bit looks up, blushes. Peck shoots the camera. The audience should see this shot on the screen.)*

LI'L BIT.   No. I don't know that.

PECK.   Listen to the music. *(Li'l Bit closes her eyes again.)* Well you are. For a thirteen year old, you have a body a twenty-year-old woman would die for.

LI'L BIT.   The boys in school don't think so.

PECK.   The boys in school are little Neanderthals in short pants. You're ten years ahead of them in maturity; it's gonna take a while for them to catch up. *(Peck clicks another shot; we see a faint smile on Li'l Bit on the screen.)*

Girls turn into women long before boys turn into men.

* See Special Note on Songs and Recordings on copyright page.

LI'L BIT.   Why is that?

PECK.   I don't know, Li'l Bit. But it's a blessing for men. *(Li'l Bit turns silent.)* Keep moving. Try arching your back on the stool, hands behind you, and throw your head back. *(The slide shows a* Playboy *model in this pose.)* Oohh, great. That one was great. Turn your head away, same position. *(Whir.)* Beautiful. *(Li'l Bit looks at him a bit defiantly.)*

LI'L BIT.   I think Aunt Mary is beautiful. *(Peck stands still.)*

PECK.   My wife is a very beautiful woman. Her beauty doesn't cancel yours out. *(More casually; he returns to the camera.)* All the women in your family are beautiful. In fact, I think all women are. You're not listening to the music. *(Peck shoots some more film in silence.)* All right, turn your head to the left. Good. Now take the back of your right hand and put in on your right cheek — your elbow angled up — now slowly, slowly, stroke your cheek, draw back your hair with the back of your hand. *(Another classic* Playboy *or Vargas.)* Good. One hand above and behind your head; stretch your body; smile. *(Another pose.)*

   Li'l Bit. I want you to think of something that makes you laugh —

LI'L BIT.   I can't think of anything.

PECK.   Okay. Think of Big Papa chasing Grandma around the living room. *(Li'l Bit lifts her head and laughs. Click. We should see this shot.)* Good. Both hands behind your head. Great! Hold that. *(From behind his camera.)* You're doing great work. If we keep this up, in five years we'll have a really professional portfolio. *(Li'l Bit stops.)*

LI'L BIT.   What do you mean in five years?

PECK.   You can't submit work to *Playboy* until you're eighteen. — *(Peck continues to shoot; he knows he's made a mistake.)*

LI'L BIT.   — Wait a minute. You're joking, aren't you, Uncle Peck?

PECK.   Heck, no. You can't get into *Playboy* unless you're the very best. And you are the very best.

LI'L BIT.   I would never do that! *(Peck stops shooting. He turns off the music.)*

PECK.   Why? There's nothing wrong with *Playboy* — it's a very classy maga —

LI'L BIT. *(More upset.)* But I thought you said I should go to college!

PECK. Wait — Li'l Bit — it's nothing like that. Very respectable women model for *Playboy* — actresses with major careers — women in college — there's an Ivy League issue every —

LI'L BIT. — I'm never doing anything like that! You'd show other people these — other *men* — these — what I'm doing. — Why would you do that?! Any *boy* around here could just pick up, just go into The Stop & Go and *buy* — Why would you ever want to — to share —

PECK. — Whoa, whoa. Just stop a second and listen to me. Li'l Bit. Listen. There's nothing wrong in what we're doing. I'm very proud of you. I think you have a wonderful body and an even more wonderful mind. And of course I want other people to *appreciate* it. It's not anything shameful.

LI'L BIT. *(Hurt.)* But this is something — that I'm only doing for you. This is something — that you said was just between us.

PECK. It is. And if that's how you feel, five years from now, it will remain that way. Okay? I know you're not going to do anything you don't feel like doing.

(He walks back to the camera.) Do you want to stop now? I've got just a few more shots on this roll —

LI'L BIT. I don't want anyone seeing this.

PECK. I swear to you. No one will. I'll treasure this — that you're doing this only for me. *(Li'l Bit, still shaken, sits on the stool. She closes her eyes.)* Li'l Bit? Open your eyes and look at me. *(Li'l Bit shakes her head no.)* Come on. Just open your eyes, honey.

LI'L BIT. If I look at you — if I look at the camera: You're gonna know what I'm thinking. You'll see right through me —

PECK. — No, I won't. I want you to look at me. All right, then. I just want you to listen. Li'l Bit. *(She waits.)* I love you. *(Li'l Bit opens her eyes; she is startled. Peck captures the shot. On the screen we see right though her. Peck says softly.)* Do you know that? *(Li'l Bit nods her head yes.)* I have loved you every day since the day you were born.

LI'L BIT. Yes. *(Li'l Bit and Peck just look at each other. Beat. Beneath the shot of herself on the screen, Li'l Bit, still looking at her uncle, begins to unbutton her blouse.*

43

A neutral Voice cuts off the above scene with:)

Implied Consent.

As an individual operating a motor vehicle in the state of Maryland, you must abide by "Implied Consent." If you do not consent to take the blood alcohol content test, there may be severe penalties: a suspension of license, a fine, community service and a possible *jail* sentence.

(The Voice shifts tone.)

Idling in the Neutral Gear.

MALE GREEK CHORUS. *(Announcing.)* Aunt Mary on behalf of her husband. *(Female Greek Chorus checks her appearance, and with dignity comes to the front of the stage and sits down to talk to the audience.)*

FEMALE GREEK CHORUS. *(As Aunt Mary.)* My husband was such a good man — is. Is such a good man. Every night, he does the dishes. The second he comes home, he's taking out the garbage, or doing yard work, lifting the heavy things I can't. Everyone in the neighborhood borrows Peck — it's true — women with husbands of their own, men who just don't have Peck's abilities — there's always a knock on our door for a jump start on cold mornings, when anyone needs a ride, or help shoveling the sidewalk — I look out, and there Peck is, without a coat, pitching in.

I know I'm lucky. The man works from dawn to dusk. And the overtime he does every year — my poor sister. She sits every Christmas when I come to dinner with a new stole, or diamonds, or with the tickets to Bermuda.

I know he has troubles. And we don't talk about them. I wonder, sometimes, what happened to him during the war. The men who fought World War II didn't have "rap sessions" to talk about their feelings. Men in his generation were expected to be quiet about it and get on with their lives. And sometimes I can feel him just fighting the trouble — whatever has burrowed deeper than the scar tissue — and we don't talk about it. I know he's having a bad spell because he comes looking for me in the house, and just hangs around me until it passes. And I keep my banter light — I discuss a new recipe, or sales, or gossip — because I think domesticity can be a balm

44

for men when they're lost. We sit in the house and listen to the peace of the clock ticking in his well-ordered living room, until it passes.

(Sharply.) I'm not a fool. I know what's going on. I wish you could feel how hard Peck fights against it — he's swimming against the tide, and what he needs is to see me on the shore, believing in him, knowing he won't go under, he won't give up —

And I want to say this about my niece. She's a sly one, that one is. She knows exactly what she's doing; she's twisted Peck around her little finger and thinks it's all a big secret. Yet another one who's borrowing my husband until it doesn't suit her anymore.

Well. I'm counting the days until she goes away to school. And she manipulates someone else. And then he'll come back again, and sit in the kitchen while I bake, or beside me on the sofa when I sew in the evenings. I'm a very patient woman. But I'd like my husband back.

I am counting the days.

(A Voice repeats:)

You and the Reverse Gear.

MALE GREEK CHORUS. Li'l Bit's Thirteenth Christmas. Uncle Peck Does the Dishes. Christmas 1964. *(Peck stands in a dress shirt and tie, nice pants, with an apron. He is washing dishes. He's in a mood we haven't seen. Quiet, brooding. Li'l Bit watches him a moment before seeking him out.)*

LI'L BIT. Uncle Peck? *(He does not answer. He continues to work on the pots.)* I didn't know where you'd gone to. *(He nods. She takes this as a sign to come in.)* Don't you want to sit with us for a while?

PECK. No. I'd rather do the dishes. *(Pause. Li'l Bit watches him.)*

LI'L BIT. You're the only man I know who does dishes. *(Peck says nothing.)* I think it's really nice.

PECK. My wife has been on her feet all day. So's your grandmother and your mother.

LI'L BIT. I know. *(Beat.)* Do you want some help?

PECK. No. *(He softens a bit towards her.)* You can help by just talking to me.

LI'L BIT.   Big Papa never does the dishes. I think it's nice.

PECK.   I think men should be nice to women. Women are always working for us. There's nothing particularly manly in wolfing down food and then sitting around in a stupor while the women clean up.

LI'L BIT.   That looks like a really neat camera that Aunt Mary got you.

PECK.   It is. It's a very nice one. *(Pause, as Peck works on the dishes and some demon that Li'l Bit intuits.)*

LI'L BIT.   Did Big Papa hurt your feelings?

PECK.   *(Tired.)* What? Oh, no — it doesn't hurt me. Family is family. I'd rather have him picking on me than — I don't pay him any mind, Li'l Bit.

LI'L BIT.   Are you angry with us?

PECK.   No, Li'l Bit. I'm not angry. *(Another pause.)*

LI'L BIT.   We missed you at Thanksgiving ... I did. I missed you.

PECK.   Well, there were ... "things" going on. I didn't want to spoil anyone's Thanksgiving.

LI'L BIT.   Uncle Peck? *(Very carefully.)* Please don't drink anymore tonight.

PECK.   I'm not ... overdoing it.

LI'L BIT.   I know. *(Beat.)* Why do you drink so much? *(Peck stops and thinks, carefully.)*

PECK.   Well, Li'l Bit — let me explain it this way. There are some people who have a ... a "fire" in the belly. I think they go to work on Wall Street or they run for office. And then there are people who have a "fire" in their heads — and they become writers or scientists or historians. *(He smiles a little at her.)* You. You've got a "fire" in the head. And then there are people like me.

LI'L BIT.   Where do you have ... a fire?

PECK.   I have a fire in my heart. And sometimes the drinking helps.

LI'L BIT.   There's got to be other things that can help.

PECK.   I suppose there are.

LI'L BIT.   Does it help — to talk to me?

PECK.   Yes. It does. *(Quiet.)* I don't get to see you very much.

LI'L BIT.   I know. *(Li'l Bit thinks.)* You could talk to me more.
PECK.   Oh?
LI'L BIT.   I could make a deal with you, Uncle Peck.
PECK.   I'm listening.
LI'L BIT.   We could meet and talk — once a week. You could just store up whatever's bothering you during the week — and then we could talk.
PECK.   Would you like that?
LI'L BIT.   As long as you don't drink. I'd meet you somewhere for lunch or for a walk — on the weekends — as long as you stop drinking. And we could talk about whatever you want.
PECK.   You would do that for me?
LI'L BIT.   I don't think I'd want Mom to know. Or Aunt Mary. I wouldn't want them to think —
PECK.   — No. It would just be us talking.
LI'L BIT.   I'll tell Mom I'm going to a girlfriend's. To study. Mom doesn't get home until six, so you can call me after school and tell me where to meet you.
PECK.   You get home at four?
LI'L BIT.   We can meet once a week. But only in public. You've got to let me — draw the line. And once it's drawn, you mustn't cross it.
PECK.   Understood.
LI'L BIT.   Would that help? *(Peck is very moved.)*
PECK.   Yes. Very much.
LI'L BIT.   I'm going to join the others in the living room now. *(Li'l Bit turns to go.)*
PECK.   Merry Christmas, Li'l Bit. *(Li'l Bit bestows a very warm smile on him.)*
LI'L BIT.   Merry Christmas, Uncle Peck.
(A Voice dictates:)

Shifting Forward from Second to Third Gear.

(The Male and Female Greek Chorus members come forward.)
MALE GREEK CHORUS.   1969. Days and Gifts: A Countdown:
FEMALE GREEK CHORUS.   A note. "September 3, 1969. Li'l Bit: You've only been away two days and it feels like months. Hope your dorm room is cozy. I'm sending you this tape cassette

— it's a new model — so you'll have some music in your room. Also that music you're reading about for class — *Carmina Burana*. Hope you enjoy. Only ninety days to go! — Peck."

MALE GREEK CHORUS.   September 22. A bouquet of roses. A note: "Miss you like crazy. Sixty-nine days ..."

TEENAGE GREEK CHORUS.   September 25. A box of chocolates. A card: "Don't worry about the weight gain. You still look great. Got a post office box — write to me there. Sixty-six days. — Love, your candy man."

MALE GREEK CHORUS.   October 16. A note: "Am trying to get through the Jane Austin you're reading — *Emma* — here's a book in return: *Liaisons Dangereuses*. Hope you're saving time for me." Scrawled in the margin the number: "47."

FEMALE GREEK CHORUS.   November 16. "Sixteen days to go! — Hope you like the perfume. — Having a hard time reaching you on the dorm phone. You must be in the library a lot. Won't you think about me getting you your own phone so we can talk?"

TEENAGE GREEK CHORUS.   November 18. "Li'l Bit — got a package returned to the P.O. Box. Have you changed dorms? Call me at work or write to the P.O. Am still on the wagon. Waiting to see you. Only two weeks more!"

MALE GREEK CHORUS.   November 23. A letter. "Li'l Bit. So disappointed you couldn't come home for the turkey. Sending you some money for a nice dinner out — nine days and counting!"

GREEK CHORUS.   *(In unison.)* November 25th. A letter:

LI'L BIT.   "Dear Uncle Peck: I am sending this to you at work. Don't come up next weekend for my birthday. I will not be here — "

(A Voice directs:)

Shifting Forward from Third to Fourth Gear.

MALE GREEK CHORUS.   December 10, 1969. A hotel room. Philadelphia. There is no moon tonight. *(Peck sits on the side of the bed while Li'l Bit paces. He can't believe she's in his room, but there's a desperate edge to his happiness. Li'l Bit is furious, edgy. There is a bottle of champagne in an ice bucket in a very nice hotel room.)*

PECK.   Why don't you sit?

LI'L BIT.   I don't want to. — What's the champagne for?

48

PECK. I thought we might toast your birthday —

LI'L BIT. — I am so pissed off at you, Uncle Peck.

PECK. Why?

LI'L BIT. I mean, are you crazy?

PECK. What did I do?

LI'L BIT. You scared the holy crap out of me — sending me that stuff in the mail —

PECK. — They were gifts! I just wanted to give you some little perks your first semester —

LI'L BIT. — Well, what the hell were those numbers all about! Forty-four days to go — only two more weeks. — And then just numbers — 69 — 68 — 67 — like some serial killer!

PECK. Li'l Bit! Whoa! This is me you're talking to — I was just trying to pick up your spirits, trying to celebrate your birthday.

LI'L BIT. My *eighteenth* birthday. I'm not a child, Uncle Peck. You were counting down to my eighteenth birthday.

PECK. So?

LI'L BIT. So? So statutory rape is not in effect when a young woman turns eighteen. And you and I both know it. *(Peck is walking on ice.)*

PECK. I think you misunderstand.

LI'L BIT. I think I understand all too well. I know what you want to do five steps ahead of you doing it. Defensive Driving 101.

PECK. Then why did you suggest we meet here instead of the restaurant?

LI'L BIT. I don't want to have this conversation in public.

PECK. Fine. Fine. We have a lot to talk about.

LI'L BIT. Yeah. We do. *(Li'l Bit doesn't want to do what she has to do.)* Could I ... have some of that champagne?

PECK. Of course, madam! *(Peck makes a big show of it.)* Let me do the honors. I wasn't sure which you might prefer — Taittingers or Veuve Clicquot — so I thought we'd start out with an old standard — Perrier Jouet. *(The bottle is popped.)*

Quick — Li'l Bit — your glass! *(Uncle Peck fills Li'l Bit's glass. He puts the bottle back in the ice and goes for a can of ginger ale.)* Let me get some of this ginger ale — my bubbly — and toast you. *(He turns and sees that Li'l Bit has not waited for him.)*

LI'L BIT. Oh — sorry, Uncle Peck. Let me have another. *(Peck fills her glass and reaches for his ginger ale; she stops him.)* Uncle Peck — maybe you should join me in the champagne.

PECK. You want me to — drink?

LI'L BIT. It's not polite to let a lady drink alone.

PECK. Well, missy, if you insist ... *(Peck hesitates.)* — Just one. It's been a while. *(Peck fills another flute for himself.)* There. I'd like to propose a toast to you and your birthday! *(Peck sips it tentatively.)* I'm not used to this anymore.

LI'L BIT. You don't have anywhere to go tonight, do you? *(Peck hopes this is a good sign.)*

PECK. I'm all yours. — God, it's good to see you! I've gotten so used to ... to ... talking to you in my head. I'm used to seeing you every week — there's so much — I don't quite know where to begin. How's school, Li'l Bit?

LI'L BIT. I — it's hard. Uncle Peck. Harder than I thought it would be. I'm in the middle of exams and papers and — I don't know.

PECK. You'll pull through. You always do.

LI'L BIT. Maybe. I ... might be flunking out.

PECK. You always think the worse, Li'l Bit, but when the going gets tough — *(Li'l Bit shrugs and pours herself another glass.)* — Hey, honey, go easy on that stuff, okay?

LI'L BIT. Is it very expensive?

PECK. Only the best for you. But the cost doesn't matter — champagne should be "sipped." *(Li'l Bit is quiet.)* Look — if you're in trouble in school — you can always come back home for a while.

LI'L BIT. *No* — *(Li'l Bit tries not to be so harsh.)* — Thanks, Uncle Peck, but I'll figure some way out of this.

PECK. You're supposed to get in scrapes, your first year away from home.

LI'L BIT. Right. How's Aunt Mary?

PECK. She's fine. *(Pause.)* Well — how about the new car?

LI'L BIT. It's real nice. What is it, again?

PECK. It's a Cadillac El Dorado.

LI'L BIT. Oh. Well, I'm real happy for you, Uncle Peck.

PECK. I got it for you.

LI'L BIT.   What?

PECK.   I always wanted to get a Cadillac — but I thought, Peck, wait until Li'l Bit's old enough — and thought maybe you'd like to drive it, too.

LI'L BIT.   *(Confused.)* Why would I want to drive your car?

PECK.   Just because it's the best — I want you to have the best. *(They are running out of "gas"; small talk.)*

LI'L BIT.	PECK.
Listen, Uncle Peck, I don't know how to begin this, but —	I have been thinking of how to say this in my head, over and over —

PECK.   Sorry.

LI'L BIT.   You first.

PECK.   Well, your going away — has just made me realize how much I miss you. Talking to you and being alone with you. I've really come to depend on you, Li'l Bit. And it's been so hard to get in touch with you lately — the distance and — and you're never in when I call — I guess you've been living in the library —

LI'L BIT.   — No — the problem is, I haven't been in the library —

PECK.   — Well, it doesn't matter — I hope you've been missing me as much.

LI'L BIT.   Uncle Peck — I've been thinking a lot about this — and I came here tonight to tell you that — I'm not doing very well. I'm getting very confused — I can't concentrate on my work — and now that I'm away — I've been going over and over it in my mind — and I don't want us to "see" each other anymore. Other than with the rest of the family.

PECK.   *(Quiet.)* Are you seeing other men?

LI'L BIT.   *(Getting agitated.)* I — no, that's not the reason — I — well, yes, I am seeing other — listen, it's not really anybody's business!

PECK.   Are you in love with anyone else?

LI'L BIT.   That's not what this is about.

PECK.   Li'l Bit — you're scared. Your mother and your grandparents have filled your head with all kinds of nonsense about men — I hear them working on you all the time — and you're scared. It won't hurt you — if the man you go to bed with really loves you. *(Li'l Bit is scared. She starts to tremble.)* And I have loved you since the day I held you in my hand. And I think everyone's just gotten you frightened to death about something that is just like breathing —

LI'L BIT.   Oh, my god — *(She takes a breath.)* I can't see you anymore, Uncle Peck. *(Peck downs the rest of his champagne.)*

PECK.   Li'l Bit. Listen. Listen. Open your eyes and look at me. Come on. Just open your eyes, honey. *(Li'l Bit, eyes squeezed shut, refuses.)* All right then. I just want you to listen. Li'l Bit — I'm going to ask you just this once. Of your own free will. Just lie down on the bed with me — our clothes on — just lie down with me, a man and a woman ... and let's ... hold one another. Nothing else. Before you say anything else. I want the chance to ... hold you. Because sometimes the body knows things that the mind isn't listening to ... and after I've held you, then I want you to tell me what you feel.

LI'L BIT.   You'll just ... hold me?

PECK.   Yes. And then you can tell me what you're feeling. *(Li'l Bit — half wanting to run, half wanting to get it over with, half wanting to be held by him.)*

LI'L BIT.   Yes. All right. Just hold. Nothing else. *(Peck lies down on the bed and holds his arms out to her. Li'l Bit lies beside him, putting her head on his chest. He looks as if he's trying to soak her into his pores by osmosis. He strokes her hair, and she lies very still. The Male Greek Chorus member and the Female Greek Chorus member as Aunt Mary come into the room.)*

MALE GREEK CHORUS.   Recipe for a Southern Boy:

FEMALE GREEK CHORUS.   *(As Aunt Mary.)* A drawl of molasses in the way he speaks.

MALE GREEK CHORUS.   A gumbo of red and brown mixed in the cream of his skin. *(While Peck lies, his eyes closed, Li'l Bit rises in the bed and responds to her aunt.)*

LI'L BIT.   Warm brown eyes —

FEMALE GREEK CHORUS.   *(As Aunt Mary.)* Bedroom eyes —

MALE GREEK CHORUS.   A dash of Southern Baptist Fire and Brimstone —

LI'L BIT.   A curl of Elvis on his forehead —

FEMALE GREEK CHORUS.   *(As Aunt Mary.)* A splash of Bay Rum —

MALE GREEK CHORUS.   A closely shaven beard that he razors just for you —

FEMALE GREEK CHORUS.   *(As Aunt Mary.)* Large hands — rough hands —

LI'L BIT.   Warm hands —

MALE GREEK CHORUS.   The steel of the military in his walk —

LI'L BIT.   The slouch of the fishing skiff in his walk —

MALE GREEK CHORUS.   Neatly pressed khakis —

FEMALE GREEK CHORUS.   *(As Aunt Mary.)* And under the wide leather of the belt —

LI'L BIT.   Sweat of cypress and sand —

MALE GREEK CHORUS.   Neatly pressed khakis —

LI'L BIT.   His heart beating Dixie —

FEMALE GREEK CHORUS.   *(As Aunt Mary.)* The whisper of the zipper — you could reach out with your hand and —

LI'L BIT.   His mouth —

FEMALE GREEK CHORUS.   *(As Aunt Mary.)* You could just reach out and —

LI'L BIT.   Hold him in your hand —

FEMALE GREEK CHORUS.   *(As Aunt Mary.)* And his mouth — *(Li'l Bit rises above her uncle and looks at his mouth; she starts to lower herself to kiss him — and wrenches herself free. She gets up from the bed.)*

LI'L BIT.   — I've got to get back.

PECK.   Wait — Li'l Bit. Did you … feel nothing?

LI'L BIT.   *(Lying.)* No. Nothing.

PECK.   Do you — do you think of me? *(The Greek Chorus whispers:)*

FEMALE GREEK CHORUS.   *(As Aunt Mary.)* Khakis —

MALE GREEK CHORUS.   Bay Rum —

FEMALE GREEK CHORUS.   *(As Aunt Mary.)* The whisper of the —

LI'L BIT.   — No. *(Peck, in a rush, trembling, gets something out of his pocket.)*

PECK.   I'm forty-five. That's not old for a man. And I haven't been able to do anything else but think of you. I can't concentrate on my work — Li'l Bit. You've got to — I want you to think about what I am about to ask you.

LI'L BIT.   I'm listening. *(Peck opens a small ring box.)*
PECK.   I want you to be my wife.
LI'L BIT.   This isn't happening.
PECK.   I'll tell Mary I want a divorce. We're not blood-related. It would be legal —
LI'L BIT.   — What have you been thinking! You are married to my aunt, Uncle Peck. She's my family. You have — you have gone way over the line. Family is family. *(Quickly, Li'l Bit flies through the room, gets her coat.)* I'm leaving. Now. I am not seeing you. Again. *(Peck lies down on the bed for a moment, trying to absorb the terrible news. For a moment, he almost curls into a fetal position.)*

I'm not coming home for Christmas. You should go home to Aunt Mary. Go home now, Uncle Peck. *(Peck gets control, and sits, rigid.)*

Uncle Peck? — I'm sorry but I have to go. *(Pause.)*

Are you all right. *(With a discipline that comes from being told that boys don't cry, Peck stands upright.)*
PECK.   I'm fine. I just think — I need a real drink. *(The Male Greek Chorus has become a bartender. At a small counter, he is lining up shots for Peck. As Li'l Bit narrates, we see Peck sitting, carefully and calmly downing shot glasses.)*
LI'L BIT.   *(To the audience.)* I never saw him again. I stayed away from Christmas and Thanksgiving for years after.

It took my uncle seven years to drink himself to death. First he lost his job, then his wife, and finally his driver's license. He retreated to his house, and had his bottles delivered. *(Peck stands, and puts his hands in front of him — almost like Superman flying.)*

One night he tried to go downstairs to the basement — and he flew down the steep basement stairs. My aunt came by weekly to put food on the porch, and she noticed the mail and the papers stacked up, uncollected.

They found him at the bottom of the stairs. Just steps away from his dark room.

Now that I'm old enough, there are some questions I would have liked to have asked him. Who did it to you, Uncle Peck? How old were you? Were you eleven? *(Peck moves to the driver's seat of the car and waits.)*

Sometimes I think of my uncle as a kind of Flying Dutchman. In the opera, the Dutchman is doomed to wander the sea; but every seven years he can come ashore, and if he finds a maiden who will love him of her own free will — he will be released.

And I see Uncle Peck in my mind, in his Chevy '56, a spirit driving up and down the back roads of Carolina — looking for a young girl who, of her own free will, will love him. Release him. *(A Voice states:)*

You and the Reverse Gear.

LI'L BIT.   The summer of 1962. On Men, Sex, and Women: Part III: *(Li'l Bit steps, as an eleven year old, into:)*

FEMALE GREEK CHORUS.   *(As Mother.)* It is out of the question. End of Discussion.

LI'L BIT.   But why?

FEMALE GREEK CHORUS.   *(As Mother.)* Li'l Bit — we are not discussing this. I said no.

LI'L BIT.   But I could spend an extra week at the beach! You're not telling me why!

FEMALE GREEK CHORUS.   *(As Mother.)* Your uncle pays entirely too much attention to you.

LI'L BIT.   He listens to me when I talk. And — and he talks to me. He teaches me about things. Mama — he knows an awful lot.

FEMALE GREEK CHORUS.   *(As Mother.)* He's a small town hick who's learned how to mix drinks from Hugh Hefner.

LI'L BIT.   Who's Hugh Hefner? *(Beat.)*

FEMALE GREEK CHORUS.   *(As Mother.)* I am not letting an eleven-year-old girl spend seven hours alone in the car with a man ... I don't like the way your uncle looks at you.

LI'L BIT.   For god's sake, mother! Just because you've gone through a bad time with my father — you think every man is evil!

FEMALE GREEK CHORUS.   *(As Mother.)* Oh no, Li'l Bit — not all men ... We ... we just haven't been very lucky with the men in our family.

LI'L BIT.   Just because you lost your husband — I still deserve a chance at having a father! Someone! A man who will look out for me! Don't I get a chance?

FEMALE GREEK CHORUS.   *(As Mother.)* I will feel terrible if something happens.

LI'L BIT.   Mother! It's in your head! Nothing will happen! I can take care of myself. And I can certainly handle Uncle Peck.

FEMALE GREEK CHORUS.   *(As Mother.)* All right. But I'm warning you — if anything happens, I hold you responsible. *(Li'l Bit moves out of this scene and toward the car.)*

LI'L BIT.   1962. On the Back Roads of Carolina: The First Driving Lesson. *(The Teenage Greek Chorus member stands apart on stage. She will speak all of Li'l Bit's lines. Li'l Bit sits beside Peck in the front seat. She looks at him closely, remembering.)*

PECK.   Li'l Bit? Are you getting tired?

TEENAGE GREEK CHORUS.   A little.

PECK.   It's a long drive. But we're making really good time. We can take the back road from here and see ... a little scenery. Say — I've got an idea — *(Peck checks his rearview mirror.)*

TEENAGE GREEK CHORUS.   Are we stopping, Uncle Peck?

PECK.   There's no traffic here. Do you want to drive?

TEENAGE GREEK CHORUS.   I can't drive.

PECK.   It's easy. I'll show you how. I started driving when I was your age. Don't you want to? —

TEENAGE GREEK CHORUS.   — But it's against the law at my age!

PECK.   And that's why you can't tell anyone I'm letting you do this —

TEENAGE GREEK CHORUS.   — But — I can't reach the pedals.

PECK.   You can sit in my lap and steer. I'll push the pedals for you. Did your father ever let you drive his car?

TEENAGE GREEK CHORUS.   No way.

PECK.   Want to try?

TEENAGE GREEK CHORUS.   Okay. *(Li'l Bit moves into Peck's lap. She leans against him, closing her eyes.)*

PECK.   You're just a little thing, aren't you? Okay — now think of the wheel as a big clock — I want you to put your right hand on the clock where three o'clock would be; and your left hand on the nine — *(Li'l Bit puts one hand to Peck's face, to stroke him. Then, she takes the wheel.)*

TEENAGE GREEK CHORUS.   Am I doing it right?

PECK.   That's right. Now, whatever you do, don't let go of the wheel. You tell me whether to go faster or slower —

TEENAGE GREEK CHORUS.   Not so fast, Uncle Peck!

PECK.   Li'l Bit — I need you to watch the road — *(Peck puts his hands on Li'l Bit's breasts. She relaxes against him, silent, accepting his touch.)*

TEENAGE GREEK CHORUS.   Uncle Peck — what are you doing?

PECK.   Keep driving. *(He slips his hands under her blouse.)*

TEENAGE GREEK CHORUS.   Uncle Peck — please don't do this —

PECK.   — Just a moment longer … *(Peck tenses against Li'l Bit.)*

TEENAGE GREEK CHORUS.   *(Trying not to cry.)* This isn't happening. *(Peck tenses more, sharply. He buries his face in Li'l Bit's neck, and moans softly. The Teenage Greek Chorus exits, and Li'l Bit steps out of the car. Peck, too, disappears.*

A Voice reflects:)

Driving in Today's World.

LI'L BIT.   That day was the last day I lived in my body. I retreated above the neck, and I've lived inside the "fire" in my head ever since.

And now that seems like a long, long time ago. When we were both very young.

And before you know it, I'll be thirty-five. That's getting up there for a woman. And I find myself believing in things that a younger self vowed never to believe in. Things like family and forgiveness.

I know I'm lucky. Although I still have never known what it feels like to jog or dance. Anything that … "jiggles." I do like to watch people on the dance floor, or out on the running paths, just jiggling away. And I say — good for them. *(Li'l Bit moves to the car with pleasure.)*

The nearest sensation I feel — of flight in the body — I guess I feel when I'm driving. On a day like today. It's five A.M. The radio says it's going to be clear and crisp. I've got five hundred miles of highway ahead of me — and some back roads too. I filled the tank last night, and had the oil checked.

Checked the tires, too. You've got to treat her … with respect.

First thing I do is: Check under the car. To see if any two year olds or household cats have crawled beneath, and strategically placed their skulls behind my back tires. *(Li'l Bit crouches.)*

Nope. Then I get in the car. *(Li'l Bit does so.)*

I lock the doors. And turn the key. Then I adjust the most important control on the dashboard — the radio — *(Li'l Bit turns the radio on: We hear all of the Greek Chorus overlapping, and static.)*

FEMALE GREEK CHORUS. *(Overlapping.)* — "You were so tiny you fit in his hand — "

MALE GREEK CHORUS. *(Overlapping.)* — "How is Shakespeare gonna help her lie on her back in the — "

TEENAGE GREEK CHORUS. *(Overlapping.)* — "Am I doing it right?" *(Li'l Bit fine-tunes the radio station. A song like "Dedicated to the One I Love"* or Orbison's "Sweet Dreams"* comes on, and cuts off the Greek Chorus.)*

LI'L BIT. Ahh … *(Beat.)* I adjust my seat. Fasten my seat belt. Then I check the right side mirror — check the left side. *(She does.)* Finally, I adjust the rearview mirror. *(As Li'l Bit adjusts the rearview mirror, a faint light strikes the spirit of Uncle Peck, who is sitting in the back seat of the car. She sees him in the mirror. She smiles at him, and he nods at her. They are happy to be going for a long drive together. Li'l Bit slips the car into first gear; to the audience.)* And then — I floor it. *(Sound of a car taking off. Blackout.)*

End of Play

---

* See Special Note on Songs and Recordings on copyright page.

PROPERTY LIST

Handkerchief (PECK)
Car keys (PECK)
Empty martini glasses (WAITER)
Swizzle sticks (WAITER)
Dinner check (WAITER)
Large bill (money) (PECK)
Lap rug (PECK)
Cookie (GRANDFATHER)
Towels (FEMALE GREEK CHORUS MEMBERS, LI'L BIT)
Tripod (PECK)
Leica camera (PECK)
Ice bucket with bottle of champagne (PECK)
Champagne glasses (LI'L BIT, PECK)
Can of ginger ale (PECK)
Small ring box (PECK)
Shot glasses (BARTENDER)

SOUND EFFECTS

Key turning ignition of car
Car revving
Beeping
Class bell
Water (shower)
Car taking off fast

NEW PLAYS

★ **ACT ONE by James Lapine.** Growing up in an impoverished Bronx family and forced to drop out of school at age thirteen, Moss Hart dreamed of joining the glamorous world of the theater. Hart's famous memoir *Act One* plots his unlikely collaboration with the legendary playwright George S. Kaufman and his arrival on Broadway. Tony Award-winning writer and director James Lapine has adapted Act One for the stage, creating a funny, heartbreaking and suspenseful celebration of a playwright and his work. "…brims contagiously with the ineffable, irrational and irrefutable passion for that endangered religion called the Theater." –NY Times. "…wrought with abundant skill and empathy." –Time Out. [8M, 4W] ISBN: 978-0-8222-3217-9

★ **THE VEIL by Conor McPherson.** May 1822, rural Ireland. The defrocked Reverend Berkeley arrives at the crumbling former glory of Mount Prospect House to accompany a young woman to England. Seventeen-year-old Hannah is to be married off to a marquis in order to resolve the debts of her mother's estate. However, compelled by the strange voices that haunt his beautiful young charge and a fascination with the psychic current that pervades the house, Berkeley proposes a séance, the consequences of which are catastrophic. "…an effective mixture of dark comedy and suspense." –Telegraph (London). "A cracking fireside tale of haunting and decay." –Times (London). [3M, 5W] ISBN: 978-0-8222-3313-8

★ **AN OCTOROON by Branden Jacobs-Jenkins. Winner of the 2014 OBIE Award for Best New American Play.** Judge Peyton is dead and his plantation Terrebonne is in financial ruins. Peyton's handsome nephew George arrives as heir apparent and quickly falls in love with Zoe, a beautiful octoroon. But the evil overseer M'Closky has other plans—for both Terrebonne and Zoe. In 1859, a famous Irishman wrote this play about slavery in America. Now an American tries to write his own. "AN OCTOROON invites us to laugh loudly and easily at how naïve the old stereotypes now seem, until nothing seems funny at all." –NY Times [10M, 5W] ISBN: 978-0-8222-3226-1

★ **IVANOV translated and adapted by Curt Columbus.** In this fascinating early work by Anton Chekhov, we see the union of humor and pathos that would become his trademark. A restless man, Nicholai Ivanov struggles to dig himself out of debt and out of provincial boredom. When the local doctor, Lvov, informs Ivanov that his wife Anna is dying and accuses him of worsening her condition with his foul moods, Ivanov is sent into a downward spiral of depression and ennui. He soon finds himself drawn to a beautiful young woman, Sasha, full of hope and energy. Finding himself stuck between a romantic young mistress and his ailing wife, Ivanov falls deeper into crisis, heading toward inevitable tragedy. [8M, 8W] ISBN: 978-0-8222-3155-4

DRAMATISTS PLAY SERVICE, INC.
440 Park Avenue South, New York, NY 10016 212-683-8960 Fax 212-213-1539
postmaster@dramatists.com www.dramatists.com

NEW PLAYS

★ **I'LL EAT YOU LAST: A CHAT WITH SUE MENGERS by John Logan.** For more than 20 years, Sue Mengers' clients were the biggest names in show business: Barbra Streisand, Faye Dunaway, Burt Reynolds, Ali MacGraw, Gene Hackman, Cher, Candice Bergen, Ryan O'Neal, Nick Nolte, Mike Nichols, Gore Vidal, Bob Fosse…If her clients were the talk of the town, she was the town, and her dinner parties were the envy of Hollywood. Now, you're invited into her glamorous Beverly Hills home for an evening of dish, dirty secrets and all the inside showbiz details only Sue can tell you. "A delectable soufflé of a solo show…thanks to the buoyant, witty writing of Mr. Logan" –NY Times. "80 irresistible minutes of primo tinseltown dish from a certified master chef." –Hollywood Reporter. [1W] ISBN: 978-0-8222-3079-3

★ **PUNK ROCK by Simon Stephens.** In a private school outside of Manchester, England, a group of highly-articulate seventeen-year-olds flirt and posture their way through the day while preparing for their A-Level mock exams. With hormones raging and minimal adult supervision, the students must prepare for their future — and survive the savagery of high school. Inspired by playwright Simon Stephens' own experiences as a teacher, PUNK ROCK is an honest and unnerving chronicle of contemporary adolescence. "[A] tender, ferocious and frightning play." –NY Times. "[A] muscular little play that starts out funny and ferocious then reveals its compassion by degrees." –Hollywood Reporter. [5M, 3W] ISBN: 978-0-8222-3288-9

★ **THE COUNTRY HOUSE by Donald Margulies.** A brood of famous and longing-to-be-famous creative artists have gathered at their summer home during the Williamstown Theatre Festival. When the weekend takes an unexpected turn, everyone is forced to improvise, inciting a series of simmering jealousies, romantic outbursts, and passionate soul-searching. Both witty and compelling, THE COUNTRY HOUSE provides a piercing look at a family of performers coming to terms with the roles they play in each other's lives. "A valentine to the artists of the stage." –NY Times. "Remarkably candid and funny." –Variety. [3M, 3W] ISBN: 978-0-8222-3274-2

★ **OUR LADY OF KIBEHO by Katori Hall.** Based on real events, OUR LADY OF KIBEHO is an exploration of faith, doubt, and the power and consequences of both. In 1981, a village girl in Rwanda claims to see the Virgin Mary. Ostracized by her schoolmates and labeled disturbed, everyone refuses to believe, until impossible happenings appear again and again. Skepticism gives way to fear, and then to belief, causing upheaval in the school community and beyond. "Transfixing." –NY Times. "Hall's passionate play renews belief in what theater can do." –Time Out [7M, 8W, 1 boy] ISBN: 978-0-8222-3301-5

DRAMATISTS PLAY SERVICE, INC.
440 Park Avenue South, New York, NY 10016 212-683-8960 Fax 212-213-1539
postmaster@dramatists.com www.dramatists.com

NEW PLAYS

★ **AGES OF THE MOON by Sam Shepard.** Byron and Ames are old friends, reunited by mutual desperation. Over bourbon on ice, they sit, reflect and bicker until fifty years of love, friendship and rivalry are put to the test at the barrel of a gun. "A poignant and honest continuation of themes that have always been present in the work of one of this country's most important dramatists, here reconsidered in the light and shadow of time passed." –NY Times. "Finely wrought...as enjoyable and enlightening as a night spent stargazing." –Talkin' Broadway. [2M] ISBN: 978-0-8222-2462-4

★ **ALL THE WAY by Robert Schenkkan. Winner of the 2014 Tony Award for Best Play.** November, 1963. An assassin's bullet catapults Lyndon Baines Johnson into the presidency. A Shakespearean figure of towering ambition and appetite, this charismatic, conflicted Texan hurls himself into the passage of the Civil Rights Act—a tinderbox issue emblematic of a divided America—even as he campaigns for re-election in his own right, and the recognition he so desperately wants. In Pulitzer Prize and Tony Award–winning Robert Schenkkan's vivid dramatization of LBJ's first year in office, means versus ends plays out on the precipice of modern America. ALL THE WAY is a searing, enthralling exploration of the morality of power. It's not personal, it's just politics. "...action-packed, thoroughly gripping... jaw-dropping political drama." –Variety. "A theatrical coup...nonstop action. The suspense of a first-class thriller." –NY1. [17M, 3W] ISBN: 978-0-8222-3181-3

★ **CHOIR BOY by Tarell Alvin McCraney.** The Charles R. Drew Prep School for Boys is dedicated to the creation of strong, ethical black men. Pharus wants nothing more than to take his rightful place as leader of the school's legendary gospel choir. Can he find his way inside the hallowed halls of this institution if he sings in his own key? "[An] affecting and honest portrait...of a gay youth tentatively beginning to find the courage to let the truth about himself become known." –NY Times. "In his stirring and stylishly told drama, Tarell Alvin McCraney cannily explores race and sexuality and the graces and gravity of history." –NY Daily News. [7M] ISBN: 978-0-8222-3116-5

★ **THE ELECTRIC BABY by Stefanie Zadravec.** When Helen causes a car accident that kills a young man, a group of fractured souls cross paths and connect around a mysterious dying baby who glows like the moon. Folk tales and folklore weave throughout this magical story of sad endings, strange beginnings and the unlikely people that get you from one place to the next. "The imperceptible magic that pervades human existence and the power of myth to assuage sorrow are invoked by the playwright as she entwines the lives of strangers in THE ELECTRIC BABY, a touching drama." –NY Times. "As dazzling as the dialogue is dreamful." –Pittsburgh City Paper. [3M, 3W] ISBN: 978-0-8222-3011-3

DRAMATISTS PLAY SERVICE, INC.
440 Park Avenue South, New York, NY 10016 212-683-8960 Fax 212-213-1539
postmaster@dramatists.com www.dramatists.com